MANUSCRIPTS AND THE TEXT
OF THE NEW TESTAMENT

MANUSCRIPTS AND THE TEXT OF THE NEW TESTAMENT

An Introduction for English Readers

by

**Keith Elliott
and
Ian Moir**

T & T CLARK
EDINBURGH

T&T CLARK LTD
59 GEORGE STREET
EDINBURGH EH2 2LQ
SCOTLAND

First published 1995

ISBN 0 567 29298 3

British Library Cataloguing-in-Publication Data
A catalogue record for this book is available from the British Library

Typeset by D & J Croal Ltd, Haddington
Printed and bound in Great Britain by Bell & Bain, Glasgow

Contents

v

Preface

Since the invention of printing, scholars have published several editions of the New Testament in Greek and a number of translations into English have appeared in print. Each of these may differ in some ways from the others, but all the copies of the same edition will offer the same text. The situation was very different in the first fourteen centuries of the Christian church, when the original books that make up the New Testament (themselves of course handwritten) were disseminated and handed down to posterity by means of manuscript copies. As individual scribes were engaged in making these copies, it is not surprising that the manuscripts we have do not present an identical text such as we have come to expect from all copies of any one printed book. Some of the differences are of great importance for the theology and interpretation of key passages.

For instance, does Luke include a reference to the Ascension in his Gospel? Some manuscripts say he does while others omit that verse. Is the famous story of the adulterous woman part of John's Gospel or not? The passage is absent in some manuscripts. In the nativity story in Luke only one Greek letter makes the difference between 'Glory to God in the highest and on earth peace, good will to men' and the alternative 'Glory to God in the highest and on earth peace to men with whom he is pleased'. Which is the original? In Romans 5:1 did Paul claim that the Christians already have peace or is peace something to be attained? Again, the manuscripts are divided. Does Mark's Gospel begin by calling Jesus 'Son of God' or not? The manuscript tradition is not in agreement. Did Mark's Gospel originally end with the report of the women's fear (according to a couple of important manuscripts) or did it include the last twelve verses (contained in the majority of manuscripts)? Was Jesus strengthened by an angel during the agony in Gethsemane or not? The verses are absent from some manuscripts.

Observant readers will find these variants (and hundreds of others) noted in the bottom margins of modern English translations of the New Testament. These editions tell us that 'Some ancient authorities' add, omit or substitute something for the text printed above. Why such variations occur in the manuscripts and the ways in which one may resolve the differences and arrive at the likeliest original reading are the prime concerns of this book.

Dr Ian Moir of Edinburgh University had it in mind to write a primer to explain textual criticism to theology students without a knowledge of Greek and general readers of the Bible similarly dependent on English translations. At the time of his sudden death in 1993 he had been working on a draft for part of the book. His widow, Kirsteen, and his family encouraged me to complete the plan. Building on the notes I inherited, I have attempted to provide a non-technical introduction to manuscripts and the New Testament text. I thank the Moir family for their trust in me to fulfil Ian's intention, and I also thank Geoffrey Green of T & T Clark for his enthusiastic encouragement. Various friends and colleagues readily agreed to comment on drafts of the book; their advice and assistance are warmly appreciated. Financial assistance from the University of Leeds is also gratefully acknowledged. I would also like to thank T. S. Pattie of the Department of Manuscripts in the British Library for his assistance in procuring some of the illustrations. Plates 1–6 are reproduced by permission of the British Library. Plate 9 is reproduced by permission of Oxford University Press, and plates 10 and 11 by permission of the Deutsche Bibelgesellschaft. Plate 12 is taken from *The Greek New Testament According to the Majority Text* copyrighted in 1985 by Thomas Nelson Inc. and is used by permission.

J. K. Elliott

List of Plates
inserted between pp. 22 and 23

Abbreviations

Abbreviations of printed English Bibles with date of British publication:

AV(KJV) Authorized (King James) Version 1611
GNB   Good News Bible 4th edition 1976
JB   Jerusalem Bible 1966
NAB   New American Bible 1970
NEB   New English Bible (New Testament) 2nd edition 1970
NIV   New International Version 1978
NRSV   New Revised Standard Version 1989
RAV   Revised Authorized Version 1982
REB   Revised English Bible 1989
RSV   Revised Standard Version 1946
RV   Revised Version 1881

Other abbreviations:

NT   New Testament
OT   Old Testament
TR   *Textus Receptus*
UBS   United Bible Societies

1

The Art of Textual Criticism

In everyday use the words 'criticism' and 'criticize' generally have a negative, pejorative sense, implying defects in the material or person criticized. One dictionary definition of 'criticize' is 'to judge (something) with disapproval, censure'. But the dictionary lists a further meaning, 'to evaluate or analyse (something)', and this is the sense in which the word is used in Biblical Studies. 'Criticism', in fact, is derived from the Greek word for judgement, and so 'criticism' could be defined as the application of judgement to a particular piece of material or a particular situation.

Textual criticism is, primarily, the study of *any* written work, the original of which no longer survives, with the purpose of recovering that original text from those copies which have chanced to survive. The reason why we need to apply textual criticism is that we are dealing with faulty texts that are the result of human activity with all its inevitable limitations. A textual critic works back from extant sources to the supposed original text from which *all* surviving copies ultimately descend. Such study is necessary for the New Testament documents. The NT books were composed in the first century AD. Printed copies of the NT have existed for only 500 years. Before the invention of printing readers relied on handwritten copies individually executed. This means that for three-quarters of the lifetime of the NT its transmission was entirely dependent on a fallible means of reproduction.

As we shall see in the next chapter, we possess nowadays more than 5,000 manuscripts containing all or part of the NT in its original language, Greek. No one manuscript represents the original text of the original authors. All that scholars can do is to work back from our extant manuscripts, in other words from copies of copies of copies. Some of the copies are old, some more recent, some are more accurate than others, some fragmentary, some

1

complete. Attempts are made to collect as many manuscripts as possible, to read them, and to compare them with each other. In this way a judgement can be reached about the originality of a given manuscript where it differs from others. And differ they do. As one can readily demonstrate in modern situations when typists are reproducing a document, all sorts of accidental slips are made. Words are misread or misunderstood; words, phrases and even whole paragraphs are omitted. The NT was not safe from such errors. This is perhaps surprising to those who assume that the copyists of sacred scripture were immune from such carelessness.

It is perhaps even more surprising to many modern readers to learn that the NT was not only subject to these normal accidental errors but also that deliberate changes were introduced to the text of the exemplars that were copied. Some changes were grammatical and linguistic. That is because readers of these texts included the educated people of their day, schooled in the Greek classics such as Homer's *Iliad* and sensitive to the style, grammar and language of the texts they were reproducing. There is no evidence that the often colloquial style of the Greek NT was improved systematically. However, it is often evident that some manuscripts conform to the Semitic, unGreek style of first-century Palestine while other manuscripts adopt a more elevated classical Greek equivalent. At other times, a text could be emended to make it agree with parallel passages, especially as the regular rereading of the texts in the church would make them familiar. Or, a reader, finding something which he failed to comprehend, could assume a mistake had been made by a previous copyist, which he then attempted to correct. Sometimes, scribes misread one word for another. Quite often the scribe's eye jumped from the word he had just copied to the same, or similar looking, set of letters later in the manuscript he was copying from, with the result that he accidentally omitted the intervening words and thereby created a shorter text. (This latter is known as homoeoteleuton, meaning that the same endings were responsible for the scribe's mistake. In some cases this technical term is not strictly accurate as the similarity of two sets of letters is not always only at the ends of words.)

Additions were also made to a text. Occasionally writers added explanatory notes to manuscripts. Such additions were made between the lines or in the margins. A copyist, finding such notes, might assume they belonged to the text but were supplied later in the exemplar from which he was working. He would then incorporate the notes as an integral part of his copy. The proofreading of copies was seldom undertaken, and these errors went undetected.

Many deliberate changes concern the meaning of a doctrinally significant passage. It has frequently been asserted that no matter of fundamental Christian doctrine is affected by textual uncertainties. That is not the case. It has to be noted that some very important passages are subject to uncertainty in the manuscripts. There is often a lack of unanimity among our surviving manuscripts in those very places which affect words, actions and statements about the status of Jesus. Even a casual flicking through the pages of a modern English edition will reveal footnotes showing variants of crucial importance. For example: Was Jesus strengthened by an angel in Gethsemane or not (Luke 22:43–44)? Does Mark call Jesus a carpenter (Mark 6:3)? Does Mark's Gospel contain a post-Easter appearance by Jesus (Mark 16:9–20)?

Again, one might be surprised that Christians took liberties with Holy Writ in this way. But it has to be remembered that in the early centuries the writings that were to make up what was to be called the NT and the Christian canon, however inspired and influential they were considered to be, did not originally have the status of scripture. The writings would not have been treated as immutable texts. They were read and used as living words.

As a result of early Christian controversies about the nature and status of Jesus during the early centuries of the church's existence, there were alterations to the texts on which these controversies were based. Many changes in our manuscripts reflect the controversies, because scribes, acting upon the instructions of the church in which and for which they worked, changed the text they were copying – often in the direction of the currently prevailing orthodoxy. The words of the NT were so important that they had to be altered if it was felt that they were wrong or ambiguous or were being misused by those deemed to be heretics. Christologically significant words were examined especially closely and were often adjusted to clarify a point in debate in favour of a particular party.

Most of these debates were raging in the first four Christian centuries. We have sufficient manuscripts from the latter part of this period, and these reveal many more differences than are to be found as innovations in later manuscripts. In fact, few later manuscripts exhibit new, theologically significant variants – they merely support readings known to us from the manuscripts of the second to fourth centuries. Orthodoxy ensured comparative stability in the text of later times. Most deliberate changes were made in the early years before canonical status was bestowed on the books that made up the NT and when Christian controversies were at their height.

This book is concerned with the differences that exist in manuscripts of the NT. How are the differences detected? What is the nature of these differences? Why do such variants occur? What can be done to resolve such differences? Can we indeed recover with a reasonable degree of confidence the original words of the NT writers?

These and other similar questions will be dealt with in the following chapters.

***

As the title to this chapter emphasizes, textual criticism is an art. It is actually both a science and an art. The collecting, classifying and collating of manuscripts is a science – a precise exercise of verifiable scholarship that can be ordered along undisputed lines. The analysis and resolution of the differences detected between manuscripts is inevitably open to debate. That is the 'art'. The debate should not be conducted subjectively. But, inevitably, there are differences in principle and emphasis among those textual critics who try to establish rules and procedures for resolving textual variation. Like all scholarly disciplines, textual criticism has evolved its own technical vocabulary. Although this introductory book attempts to avoid technical terms, they cannot be ignored completely. The Glossary at the end of the book is recommended as a convenient point of reference if an unfamiliar term appears.

In the next chapter we shall look at the sources for establishing the text of the NT. Chapter 3 looks at ways in which the text has been, and can be, edited. Chapter 4 is the longest section and is devoted to practical examples of particular, selected variants, all of which are to be found in the footnotes of modern editions. Much of that chapter will be concerned with looking at significant variants due to omission, addition and change. It is not possible to deal with more than a representative sample of the most interesting or important differences, but it is to be hoped that readers will go on to look at other variants and to apply their own judgement to the merits of one variant over another, and not necessarily accept blindly the decisions of editor and translator. All the variants in Chapter 4 are discussed without requiring the reader to have a knowledge of Greek.

Not all the examples in Chapter 4 lend themselves to a neat solution: often, competing arguments make total certainty impossible. Professional textual critics themselves often disagree even when they aim to apply the same principles. Professor B. M. Metzger has written a companion volume on the textual variations in the United Bible Societies' text, entitled *A Textual Commentary on the Greek New Testament,* in which he summarizes a number of the text-critical decisions reached by the members of the committee of editors. That committee tended to favour certain early manuscripts, a good geographical spread of manuscripts, and convincing reasons why one reading gave rise to the secondary, alternative readings. Sometimes this so-called reasoned eclecticism does not yield a clear decision, particularly when the favoured manuscripts are divided, some supporting one reading, some another, or when the arguments based on criteria such as the author's style seem to be leading to a reading supported by only a few manuscripts. Under circumstances such as these, it can be seen from that book that the scholars on the committee disagreed among themselves and frequently had to reach a majority verdict about what was to be the reading to be adopted in the text. Sometimes, when the dispute concerned the choice between including or excluding a certain word or words, they had to resolve their disagreements by enclosing the disputed word or passage in single (or, occasionally, double) square brackets.

There are other Greek New Testaments which are fundamentally opposed to the principles behind the UBS edition. Some of them follow the majority of manuscripts, and publish a text not unlike the one that lies behind the NT part of the Authorized Version.

The co-author of the present book, J. K. Elliott, is identified with an approach to textual criticism that prefers to accept as original a reading that can be defended primarily on grounds such as language, style and usage, and he pays scant attention to the number and alleged weight of the manuscripts supporting it. This primer is not the place to promote one approach over another; in the examples discussed in Chapter 4 an attempt will be made to keep the discussion as objective and open as possible.

Before we turn to sources and the methods of NT textual criticism, it is worth drawing attention to a few points:

1. Throughout this book we do well to remember that, once the canon was established, every single manuscript of the Greek NT was the authoritative canonical text used by the Christians who owned it. Few ancient readers would have had access to more than one manuscript. If their version of Mark contained the final twelve verses (Mark 16:9–20) then for them those words were authoritative. Similarly if they owned a copy that lacked the story of the adulteress (normally numbered John 7:53 – 8:11) then they would be unaware of this piece of Christian teaching as part of their Bible.

2. Another thing to bear in mind is that every variation in the text ultimately originated with one manuscript incorporating the change. (It could be suggested in a few cases that particular errors may have been created coincidentally and independently in more than one copy.) Once a change had been introduced, be it omission, addition, substitution or a differing word order, then all subsequent copies made from that altered manuscript would perpetuate the change, whereas manuscripts copied from the unaltered copy would retain the original author's wording. When assembling textual variants we tend to report that reading 1 is supported by *x* number of manuscripts and variant 2 by *y* number, and reading 3 is found in, say, only a couple of witnesses. What we are really indicating is that our extant fund of NT manuscripts has thrown up three choices, one of which probably represents the original text, and is the ancestor of the changes found in the alternatives. We shall return to this topic again in Chapter 3. It is a worthy principle of textual criticism to accept as original the reading that best explains itself as the origin of any variants. The decision should not be based on the number or date of surviving manuscripts supporting each reading.

3. Throughout this book we assume that it is possible and practicable to recreate the original words of the NT authors. No one surviving manuscript can be relied on to give us that original text on its own. Unfortunately, all our manuscripts are contaminated with corruptions. But, fortunately, with so many and so varied a fund

of manuscripts, the original text has most probably lived on in some of these copies. The task of the textual critic is to find where the original reading lies at each and every point of divergence in the manuscripts, and, ideally, to try to explain how and why the variant or variants arose in the first place. Related to this is point 4 following.

4. The number of manuscripts and the antiquity of many of them place the NT textual critic in a position envied by scholars attempting to edit the Greek and Latin classics. For many of these works the number of surviving manuscripts is very small and none of their extant manuscripts are as close in time to the originals as the early NT manuscripts are to their autographs. As a result, many editors of the classics are obliged from time to time to resort to guesses when the manuscripts fail to reveal a sensible reading. Conjectural emendation has, nevertheless, been applied to the NT, and we shall be returning to this in the Postscript. But it is worth stating now that unless a foolproof case can be made that all of the many surviving manuscripts have failed to preserve the original text, then it should not be necessary to resort to guesswork which can lead to a modern rewriting of the NT text.

5. The confident assumption that the original text is there to be uncovered is the motive of all mainstream textual criticism and it depends on two other assumptions.

a) One is that each NT book was issued in a definitive edition as the final published text. Matthew, for example, wrote his Gospel after a long literary process in which he assimilated material from many sources; he adapted previous written accounts but finally issued a finished Gospel as his own work. Paul, likewise, issued his letters after a gestation period in which he may indeed have attempted a few first drafts. It is literary criticism that concerns itself with an author's sources and composition. Textual criticism begins once the author's task is done and the book issued. We no longer have the autographs: the epistles Paul himself sent have long since disappeared, the copy of the Gospel Matthew personally wrote is now no more. All we have are copies of copies of copies, and it is from some of those copies that textual critics work backwards, recording any changes they see in the manuscripts, trying to explain the reasons for the alterations, and from the mixture of alternatives to identify what belonged to the original issued text and what is secondary. If archaeology were ever to unearth the long-lost original autographs then the primary purpose of textual criticism would be achieved, and all the textual critic would be left to do would be to plot where manuscripts preserved that original and where each went wrong. But such a find has not happened yet.

b) Each author published only one version of his work. There are complicating factors if literary critics can build up a good case for believing that Luke issued two different editions of his Book of Acts. But, in general, we may legitimately assume that each of the NT books was originally published in one finalized form only, and it is that which the text critic is trying to re-establish.

6. Most modern textual critics can agree on the bulk of the text (some 95 per cent of it, perhaps). It is the remaining 5 per cent or so where disputes occur and differing conclusions may be found. These discrepancies are the cause for most of the variants to be seen in the footnotes of our translations.

7. There are a few textual critics who are sceptical of our ever getting behind the text groupings that can be detected in the second and third centuries, but most textual critics are relatively optimistic that one can reach back to the texts of the 1st century.

8. Textual criticism is important. Commentaries, exegetical studies, translators, preachers and teachers and all who refer to the text of the NT need to be convinced that their edition of the text is reliable. Where complete certainty over the originality of the text is impossible or is not achievable, then to have the most important alternatives available in footnotes is a helpful requirement. Footnotes or a critical apparatus, far from being an unnecessary intrusion, are an essential part of an honest display of the evidence available. All readers should be encouraged to exercise their own intelligence and recognize that sometimes what appears to be a reading relegated to the sidelines is worthy of consideration as a reading that should stand in the text. There is no justification for assuming that an editor or translator is always 100 per cent certain and that their judgements are final.

2

The New Testament in Greek

The books of the NT were originally written in Greek, and although the original manuscripts in the handwriting of Paul, Matthew, Luke and the other authors are not extant, many manuscripts descended from these autographs have survived and are, in general, accessible in various libraries, monasteries and other collections. The largest holdings of manuscripts are housed in libraries in Athens, Oxford, Paris, London, St Petersburg and the Vatican, and in the monasteries on Mount Athos.

One problem for NT textual critics is not the dearth of material but the wealth of sources demanding their attention. There exist more than 5,000 manuscripts containing all or part of the NT in Greek. Actually only about sixty are complete New Testaments. Mostly what was copied was only a portion of the NT; that is, one manuscript, for example, might contain the Gospels, another the Pauline corpus, another the book of Revelation.

In addition to the manuscripts in the original language, there are large numbers of manuscripts in Latin (some 10,000), in Coptic, in Syriac; the NT was translated at an early date into these languages. They, as well as later translations into Armenian, Georgian, Ethiopic, and Gothic, can often aid our understanding of the underlying Greek.

The majority of the Greek manuscripts have been microfilmed; these films are deposited at the Institute for New Testament Textual Research at the University of Münster in Germany. This means that those wishing to study NT manuscripts nowadays can consult copies of most of them in one place.

Some NT manuscripts are complete, others contain only a few verses, or even parts of only a few words, where sufficient remains to allow a proper identification of what is left as a biblical fragment. What is probably the earliest fragment is in Manchester and is classified in the official register, maintained in Münster, as

Papyrus 52. It contains only a few verses of John's Gospel and there is general agreement that it was written no later than the middle of the second century AD, in other words relatively soon after the actual date of composition of this Gospel. The date of the fragment is sometimes given as 125 AD but, of course, this does not mean that the papyrus is actually dated. The precise dating of biblical papyri is notoriously difficult; occasionally one hears claims that some of the NT papyri should be dated earlier than the original editors proposed.

Early documents are usually dated by their handwriting, characteristics of which provide certain datable clues, although precision is not always possible. In the early days of papyrology (the scientific study of papyri manuscripts) it was thought that, as Christianity seems to have penetrated Egypt rather slowly, it was improbable that any Christian papyri would be found earlier than the third century AD. Later, however, papyri came to light which showed unmistakable signs, on palaeographical grounds, of having been written earlier than this, and there are now several which scholars would assign to the second century. Others think this tendency has gone too far, but the primacy of the Manchester fragment is still generally unquestioned.

There are good examples of early manuscripts from the second century onwards, although, as one would expect, the majority of our 5,000 Greek manuscripts are medieval, and date from the eleventh century up to the time of the invention of printing. About 95 per cent of extant manuscripts were written after the eighth century, that is to say, seven centuries or more elapse between the originals and the bulk of our surviving copies. The date of the manuscript, however, does not mean that the text it contains is from that date, so a late manuscript could have a very early text. A scribe in the tenth century, say, could have been copying from a third-century exemplar.

The extant Greek NT manuscripts come in all shapes and sizes. Some are of small format and are likely to have been pocket books for private devotion at home; others were de luxe editions written for wealthy churches – a few of these are on purple parchment with silver ink. Some are written on papyrus, others on parchment. Some are profusely illustrated. Some have one column per page, others are in double or treble columns. We know that the Emperor Constantine in the fourth century commissioned fifty NT manuscripts to be written on fine parchment by professional scribes. There is no proof that any of those fifty survive, but this decree shows that officially instigated copies were made; it is to be assumed that such patronage would have ensured high standards. Most manuscripts, however, were probably individually produced copies made locally on the authority of leading Christians.

Some manuscripts are bilinguals, Greek–Latin, Greek–Coptic, for example. These are of great interest because of what they tell us about language equivalents and also because they show how the original Greek was understood at the time the ancestors of these bilinguals were written. Mention may be made of two famous bilingual manuscripts, both apparently hailing from the Middle East and both at one time in the possession of Theodore Beza, the Swiss Reformer. One is Codex Bezae now containing the Gospels and Acts and a few verses of 3 John. (There is more on this manuscript later in this chapter.) The other manuscript is the equally aberrant manuscript of the Pauline epistles known as Codex Claromontanus. This manuscript, named after Clermont in France, is now in Paris; it is in a very worn and fragile state, but it also bears witness to many of the variations to be found in other bilingual manuscripts.

Another source of information for the textual critic comes from patristic commentaries. Apart from the many manuscripts of commentaries and treatises by the church Fathers which exist in Greek, Latin and other languages, there exist not a few biblical manuscripts which contain on the same page the Greek NT text together with marginal commentaries from patristic sources. Here we often find the NT quoted in lemmata (that is, sections which differ from the actual text on the same page). Sometimes the commentary refers to the text and shows that the commentator knows one or more variant readings which he quotes.

NT manuscripts are usually in codex (book) form not rolls. There is a strong case for arguing that Christians were responsible for popularizing, if not inventing, the codex. One possible incentive for their revolutionizing the format of publication was that they wished originally to publish their four chosen Gospels together and this was practical only if the codex form was adopted. (It was impracticable to contain the four Gospels on one roll.) There are over forty papyrus fragments containing the text of the Gospels, many from the second and third centuries. Nearly all of these come from a codex not a roll whereas for non-Christian papyri the roll dominated until the fourth century.

The papyrus fragment containing Hebrews known as Papyrus 13 (see Plate 1) is written on the back of a reused roll. This is a well-established method of saving writing material: an old parchment roll, no longer required, was used on the outside. It is known as an opisthograph (i.e. written on the back).

In the case of a codex, recycling also occurred. An old manuscript could be scraped clean and used over again for another work. In some instances enough of the erased original is left to allow it to be deciphered in whole or in part. But often a manuscript was reused without the new writer bothering to clean off the original writing. Sometimes the new writing was placed in the interlinear spaces of the original manuscript, or sometimes the manuscript was turned upside down and overwritten, or, again, the manuscript was turned at right angles and rewritten across the original. Such a manuscript is known as a palimpsest (from the Greek 'to rub again' – meaning that the manuscript has twice been cleaned to take writing, although many so-called palimpsests are merely overwritten texts). A few NT manuscripts are palimpsests where the original writing is the biblical text which has been overwritten; other NT palimpsests have the biblical writing on the top and a non-biblical work underneath. Palimpsests are not easy to read and not a few were damaged at the end of the nineteenth century by the use of chemical reagents to help the visibility of the ink. Modern study uses ultraviolet lamps. Infrared photography has also been used in some instances with considerable success to help in the process of decipherment.

****

The official register, maintained at the Institute for New Testament Textual Research at the University of Münster, classifies manuscripts into two groups: I) lectionaries and II) continuous-text manuscripts. This division is by function: the latter group of manuscripts are separated from those in which the text was rearranged to meet the lectionary needs of the church calendar.

I) By the fourth century various churches had established their own systems of lessons for use in monastic reading, in public worship and, so far as it was feasible, in private study. Thus, the custom arose of producing manuscripts not containing the whole

NT in its natural sequence, but confined to the appointed lessons for the ecclesiastical year. The lectionaries are catalogued with an italic letter l followed by a number. The highest lectionary number is now $l\,2403$. Some lectionaries are on paper; most, however, are on parchment.

II) The continuous-text manuscripts are further divided. i) First by writing material. Those written on papyrus are catalogued as P followed by a number. The highest number to date is P^{99} and all are dated pre-eighth century – most in the third to fourth centuries. They are thereby separated from the rest of the manuscripts; which are written on parchment. ii) The parchment manuscripts are divided into a) those written in upper case letters, which are known as uncials or majuscules, and b) those written in a cursive script, which are known as either cursives or minuscules. Uncials are written in lines of continuous script without divisions between words. Cursive script is like modern handwriting, with some individual letters of a word joined. (The regular separation of words was achieved by the late Middle Ages.)

Uncial script was the preferred method of writing up to the ninth century (and, of course, the papyri are in an uncial hand). Cursive handwriting gradually replaced this from the seventh century onwards. The parchment uncials are listed with a number prefixed by 0 (0306 is the highest number registered so far) although the earliest numbered parchment uncials in the catalogue are also known by a capital letter from the Greek or Roman alphabet and, in one case, by the first letter of the Hebrew alphabet (aleph). It would be convenient if nowadays only the numbers were used in listings and discussions, but for historical reasons the older lettering survives. Some scholars use both forms e.g. B 03. The cursives are numbered from 1 onwards, reaching at the moment 2856. If one looks at the footnotes of a scholarly edition of the Greek NT one finds the manuscript sigla (i.e. the symbols, letters or numbers) printed in support of each variant. (See Plate 10.) It is thus a convenient and unambiguous shorthand way of referring to a particular textual witness.

The highest numbers in the register above do not tell us the precise quantity of separate manuscripts available. Occasionally, the same manuscript was found to have been registered twice: when that was discovered, one of the numbers was deleted.

Sometimes two or more fragmentary manuscripts were

subsequently found to have come from the same manuscript, and thus numbers were made redundant. In some cases, a registered manuscript is no longer extant; war and fire account for the loss of a few manuscripts. After deducting such losses the total number of papyri is 97, uncials about 270, cursives about 2,747, and lectionaries about 2,310. These totals vary as year by year adjustments are made to the lists by occasional additions and refinements.

Let us now look at some manuscripts a) on papyrus and b) on parchment.

Papyri

Papyri are made from the pith of the papyrus plant, *Cyperus Papyrus L*, a sedge which grew in great profusion in the Nile Valley. By laying strips of its pith lengthways and covering them with lengths laid over them at right angles, a durable and cheap writing material was produced. The two layers were pressed together, dried, and trimmed. Sheets could be pasted together. Rolls or codexes could then be manufactured. Although the surfaces were sometimes smoothed with pumice, it was obviously easier to write on the side where the grain was from side to side (commonly called the recto) than the side where the writing would go against the grain (commonly called the verso). In NT manuscripts both sides were usually written on. Although all our papyri are fragmentary, some are relatively extensive: 102 of the original 144 pages of P^{75}, containing Luke and John, are extant; 86 of the original 104 pages of P^{46} survive.

Papyrus 46 (P^{46}), containing Paul's letters, was found in Egypt and is now part of the Chester Beatty Collection. Other NT manuscripts in that collection include most of P^{45} (with extensive portions of the Gospels and Acts), P^{47} (containing chapters of Revelation), P^{97} (with a few verses of Luke), and P^{99} (a lexicon based on portions of Romans, 2 Corinthians, Galatians and Ephesians). Chester Beatty began acquiring biblical manuscripts in the 1930s, largely through dealers in Egypt. Many of the biblical manuscripts in his collection were edited with photographic plates by Sir Frederic Kenyon.

The famous P^{75} belongs to the collection founded by Martin Bodmer, as do P^{72}, containing the letters of Peter and Jude in a single codex, P^{73}, with fragments of Matthew, and P^{74}, with extensive portions of Acts and the Catholic Epistles. Arguably the most important is P⁶⁶ containing John's Gospel. It dates from c.200 AD and is in a remarkably good state of preservation. No study of the text of John is complete without taking this manuscript into account, partly because of the many significant corrections it contains.

Many of these fragmented books were divided up when middlemen and dealers in the Middle East sold off to buyers only parts of the papyri that came into their hands. That is why portions of the same book are sometimes now to be found in more than one location. The provenance and precise history of how and where many of these texts were discovered are often shrouded in mystery.

Both Martin Bodmer and Sir Chester Beatty were wealthy and successful bibliophiles and collectors; between them they managed to get hold of the most significant NT papyri available. Each built a library to accommodate his precious possessions. The Bodmer Library is in Cologny, a suburb of Geneva; the Chester Beatty Library is in Dublin.

Many other papyrus manuscripts have been excavated in Oxyrhynchus in Egypt. The large waste dumps there have revealed numerous literary and non-literary papyri, all of which are systematically examined, and many have been subsequently published in an ongoing series. The published fragments include some thirty NT manuscripts.

A separate science has been developed for the study of this material, which has also preserved classical prose and poetical works in Greek and also many archive documents in a variety of languages. This science is known as papyrology and it has made extensive contributions to our understanding of the text of the NT.

The third to fourth-century P¹³, containing part of the epistle to the Hebrews, is reproduced as Plate 1.

Parchment

Papyrus was gradually replaced by parchment – a material produced by dressing and polishing animal skins. In many cases they, like the papyri, are badly damaged and the science of palaeography (study of ancient writing) seeks to repair the damage and to determine the lost text.

UNCIALS ON PARCHMENT

Among the uncials, four have had a disproportionate influence on editors of the text of the NT in the past century.

1. Aleph or 01 or Codex Sinaiticus, so called because it was discovered at St Catherine's Monastery on Mount Sinai. (See Plate 6.) The circumstances of its discovery by Constantin von Tischendorf, his subsequent publication of its text, his donation of the manuscript to the Tsar of Russia, its sale to the British Museum in 1933 (since when it may be seen in the British Library's Department of Manuscripts on permanent display) all served to keep its name in the public eye. Many non-specialists were also aware of the somewhat underhand way in which Tischendorf persuaded the monks of St Catherine's to part with their manuscript. The claim in the mid-nineteenth century by a notorious Greek adventurer, Simonides, that he himself had forged the manuscript also focused attention on Tischendorf's discovery among the literary public. But above all, it was the fact that this was the oldest complete Greek NT found that made scholars from the time of its first discovery heed its text. Tischendorf himself re-edited his own published Greek NT to take account of its readings. Westcott and Hort praised the quality of its text and took it into their Greek NT of 1881. Codex Sinaiticus dates from the fourth century. In addition to the NT and most of the OT, it contains the epistle of Barnabas and the Shepherd of Hermas. It is written in four columns per page and is the only NT manuscript written in this way. (See Plates 2 and 3.)

2. A or 02 of the fifth century, known as Codex Alexandrinus, contains most of the NT together with most of the OT and 1–2 Clement. The manuscript was presented to King Charles I of England in 1627 by the Orthodox Patriarch of Constantinople. It is written in two columns and its text seems to have been created from several different exemplars. It was found in Alexandria, and, like Sinaiticus, is on permanent display in the British Library. (See Plate 4.)

3. B or 03 is known as Codex Vaticanus because it is deposited in the Vatican Library. It is a fourth-century manuscript and has extensive coverage of the NT and OT. It is this manuscript above all others that influenced the Greek NT published by Westcott and Hort in 1881 (and also the English Revised Version of the same year) as well as most subsequent editions of the NT in Greek. It appealed to many nineteenth-century scholars because they thought its brevity was indicative of its closeness to the original.

4. D or 05 is known as Codex Bezae after Theodore Beza who donated the manuscript in 1581 to the Cambridge University Library, where it may still be seen. As we noted earlier, this is a bilingual manuscript – with Greek and Latin on facing pages. It is an early manuscript (fifth or even fourth century) and contains the Gospels, most of Acts and a portion of 3 John. It is the main representative of the wrongly named Western text (a term to be found in Chapter 4 in the discussion on the selected variant readings). One characteristic of this text is that it frequently differs from most other Greek witnesses, although it has support from the early, pre-Jerome Latin, especially in the book of Acts. The Western text of Acts is about a tenth longer than the usual printed text and many of the additions there are found in D 05. It can be shown that most of these variants are older than the manuscript, Codex Bezae, itself and this raises interesting questions about whether they are more original than, or at least contemporary with, the text which we usually read. Most critics consider this manuscript to be a mere maverick displaying an aberrant text, but an increasing number of scholars now recognizes D 05 to be a representative of an earlier, i.e. second century, form of the original text, and therefore one whose readings must be considered carefully if one is hoping to get back to the earliest and possibly original form of the NT itself. We shall discuss later the possibility that the distinctive text of D in Acts may represent an alternative form of that book prepared by Luke himself. The variants in D are therefore prominent in any discussion of the text and its readings are regularly recorded in the footnotes of the critical editions of the Greek NT.

CURSIVES

Individual cursives have not been accorded the same attention as the famous papyri or uncials. But cursive 33 was once called 'the queen of the cursives', and is regularly cited in the critical apparatuses. Some other minuscules are included fairly regularly. These include 424, 579, 1881 and the cursives which make up Family 1 and Family 13 (see the final section of this chapter). Cursive 1739 is an important witness for Acts. Cursive 699 is reproduced as Plate 5.

***

The following diagram summarizes the above:

Greek manuscripts

→ ninth century	seventh century →
written in upper case (uncials)	written in lower case (cursives)
PAPYRUS	Family 1
P^{13} P^{45}	Family 13
P^{46} P^{47}	33 424
P^{66} P^{72} P^{73}	579 699
P^{74} P^{75} P^{97} P^{99}	1739 1881
PARCHMENT	
Sinaiticus	
Alexandrinus	
Vaticanus	
Bezae	

***

Chapter 5 on the history of textual criticism shows that our knowledge of NT manuscripts has grown over recent centuries. Most scholarly enterprises involved in gathering manuscripts into private collections, university and state libraries have occurred in the West only in the last 200 years. Journeys to the monasteries and libraries of Greece and the Middle East, facilitated by modern means of transport, resulted in the cataloguing, filming, reading, collating, and in some cases the removal of manuscripts. Archaeological excavations in the twentieth century have also been responsible for our knowledge of nearly all the papyri as well as other finds.

Various methods of describing and referring to manuscripts deposited in recognized collections were devised. Apart from an individual library's own classification system of numbering its holdings, the generally accepted reference numbering for NT Greek manuscripts is the one established by Caspar René Gregory in 1908. It has been maintained more recently by Kurt Aland in Münster. Hence it is now usual to call it the Gregory-Aland system. If anyone discovers a new NT manuscript, the convention is to have it formally accepted and included in that officially recognized register.

The contents of some manuscripts, especially the earliest, are described in learned journals and in scholarly works. These publications usually include photographs and collations. But most manuscripts are never published in full. That is because most of them do not yield sufficient or significant differences from previously known manuscripts to merit such detailed attention as a matter of priority. The reason is that the bulk of our known manuscripts are, inevitably, medieval cursives, which by and large conform to the standardized text of the Byzantine Church. Obviously there are exceptions and all medieval manuscripts are sampled by the Institute for New Testament Textual Research in the University of Münster from their microfilm holdings, in order to check if a manuscript merits fuller study and an exhaustive collation. What they have done is to select a fixed number of significant places in the NT text where there are important differences in the manuscript traditions, and then to check whether the manuscript under investigation conforms to the conventional reading of the Byzantine manuscripts (known as the Majority Text) or whether it is regularly out of step. If it does betray significant divergences from the Majority Text, then that manuscript is earmarked as deserving thoroughgoing study.

Collations

A collation is the comparison of a manuscript against a recognized norm and is an exercise undertaken in order to reveal the distinctive features of manuscripts. Where a manuscript is to be read in full, the convention is to collate it against a recognized printed edition of the Greek NT (traditionally the so-called *Textus Receptus* – described in the Glossary at the end of the book – has been used, although other editions such as Westcott and Hort's text of 1881 have served the purpose). The reason for reading a manuscript against another text is to enable differences to be identified, isolated and collected. Other, more sophisticated, methods have been devised, in which collations are made against a wide spectrum of manuscripts in order to enable scholars to identify whether any readings of the manuscript under investigation are allied with other, previously collated, manuscripts. In that way the profile of a manuscript can be established. Computers are now being used to assist in this work. (See Postscript.)

Variants and the Critical Apparatus

When a manuscript displays any significant differences its readings may be included in the footnotes of a printed edition, or its evidence added to an already known variant. In English editions the manuscripts are not cited: normally the footnotes say 'Some ancient authorities here add/omit . . .' or 'Some manuscripts read . . .', but in Greek scholarly editions the actual manuscripts are identified by their number or siglum. The footnotes in a Greek testament can look rather forbidding but the introductory pages of the edition usually explain all its abbreviations and symbols. The aim of all these sigla is to keep the scale of the footnotes to manageable proportions. Even so, some editions look rather bottom heavy as the footnotes become greater than the basic printed text. The footnotes in the Greek NT, as in all such literature, are usually called the critical apparatus or, in Latin, *apparatus criticus.*

Readers who wish to graduate to a Greek NT to consult its apparatus will need to familiarize themselves with the conventions used by the editors. The introductions to the United Bible Societies' *Greek New Testament* or to Nestle-Aland, *Novum Testamentum Graece*, which are the two most widely used editions today, have commendably helpful and informative introductory matter, as well as an outline of the principles underlying the edition. These two editions are listed in the Bibliography at the end of this book. All manuscripts found in their apparatuses are listed. An exhaustive catalogue of the complete register of Greek NT manuscripts is also published: K. Aland, *Kurzgefasste Liste der griechischen Handschriften des Neuen Testaments* (Berlin: de Gruyter,[2] 1994).

However full the critical apparatus of a Greek NT may look, it contains only a sample of all the differences between manuscripts. The latest edition of the Nestle-Aland text prints some 15,000 variants. The United Bible Societies have limited their apparatus to those variants deemed to be of importance to translators and as a result it has only about 1,440 variants. More complete scholarly editions have been produced, most notably the nineteenth century edition by Tischendorf (see Plate 7). Hermann Freiherr von Soden, whose name also appears in our historical sketch (Chapter 5) produced a very full apparatus (see Plate 8). The International Greek New Testament Project has published a full apparatus to Luke's Gospel, and is at present at work on a similar apparatus to John (see Postscript). In this edition the text of the verse of the Gospel preceding each portion of apparatus is merely a convenient collating base, namely the *Textus Receptus.* (A reduced page of the Project's edition of Luke appears as Plate 9.) No exhaustive apparatus exists for Luke or for any biblical book for that matter, although it is conceivable that computers could store electronically such an apparatus. It may be unnecessary, and it is certainly too expensive, to print all this out as a book publication. It has been estimated that there are some 300,000 variants in all manuscripts read to date. Obviously many of these may be mere spelling slips and careless errors which are not substantive and meaningful variants. Orthographical variants (that is, changes in spelling), may have a place if one is assessing scribal habits, the characteristics of the manuscript in question, or the history of written Greek, but, in general, they are of limited interest and importance to the average interpreter and reader of a Greek testament.

In a modern language translation, of course, only those variants that are considered to affect the meaning of the text are included in the footnotes. Some English editions have a fairly wide-ranging set of text-critical notes. The NRSV has about 500. The JB is also well furnished with textual footnotes. The RAV also has a high number of variants indicated, especially those showing where the AV differs from modern texts. Other translations, like the NIV and GNB, also alert their readers to textual variants at selected points.

Whether we are dealing with a Greek text or an English translation, the editors use the device of the footnotes for various reasons. Sometimes, the variant reading is offered as a genuine alternative to the text printed: the editors are unsure which reading represents the original and resolve the dilemma by displaying to their readers the choice on offer. In other words, the reader is invited to contribute to the debate. This invitation means that one should not disregard the alternatives in the footnotes, but consider them as potentially original. At other times, the editors themselves might be quite clear that their chosen printed text is the original reading, but nonetheless print in the footnotes a variant which is interesting in its own right. This is especially likely if in the past it was the reading found in influential editions or translations, such as the Greek *Textus Receptus* or the English AV, or which had an impact on the history of the church or Christian doctrine.

Versions and Fathers

A critical apparatus to a Greek NT usually contains, in addition to the evidence of Greek manuscript witnesses, the evidence of the ancient versions. This can often bolster our knowledge and give a clue to the antiquity or geographical spread of a particular variant. If a reading found in only a few Greek manuscripts is supported by the evidence of, say, the Coptic, Latin and Syriac that reading is not only likely to be an old reading, but obviously one that was widely known. In theory a version can point to an original reading for which no Greek manuscript evidence is known. Readings in some of the versions, such as Syriac or Latin, may be older than in any surviving Greek manuscripts. There are clearly problems in handling the NT text in a language other than Greek when attempting to establish the text of the Greek. Certain versional readings are, of course, the creations of that version. But when we are looking at alterations that concern a longer text versus a shorter text, the variants in Greek can often be legitimately supported by a version.

In addition, an apparatus can display the names of church Fathers. The famous writers in the early church, Augustine, Origen, Jerome and many more, quoted the scriptures in their sermons, homilies and commentaries. We do not know which biblical manuscripts they possessed and used, so their testimony is an indirect way of gaining access to a greater number of otherwise unknown manuscripts. Patristic testimony, like versional, can help us identify the antiquity and geographical location of a text, because we know when and where the Fathers wrote. Obviously one must be cautious in citing patristic testimony, and one must, of course, be doubly careful with those Fathers who were not writing in Greek. A Father may not have been accurate in his citations, or may have been

1. Papyrus 13 showing Hebrews 2:14 – 3:9.

2. Codex Sinaiticus folio 272 showing 1 Corinthians 12:15 – 14:5. The omission (through homoeoteleuton) of the words 'I have become a noisy gong . . . but do not have love' (13:1–2) has been made good in the top margin by a corrector.

CENCⲰMAIⲰYCE
POYMENⲰIⲧEPIC·
IEPANAOYCTIMH
INAMHHCXICMA
TACNTⲰCⲰMATI
AⲖⲖATOAYTOYⲧE
PAⲖⲖHⲖⲰNMEPI
MNⲰCITAMEⲖH
KAIEITEIIACXEIN
MEⲖOCCYNIIACXEI
IIANTATAMEⲖH
EITEⲖOCAZETAⲓⲘ
ⲖOCCYⲅXAIPEIIIA
TATAMEⲖH
YMEICⲀEECTECⲰ
MAXYKAIMEⲖHK
MEPOYCKAIOYCM
EOETOOOCENTHK
KAHCIAIIPⲰTON
AIIOCTOⲖOYC
ⲖEYTEPON
IIPOФHTAC
TPITON
ⲀIⲀACKAⲖOYC
EIIEITAⲖYNAMIC
EIIEITAXAPICMA
TAIAMATⲰN
ANTIⲖHMⲧEIC
KYBEPNHCICIⲬⲀⲆ·
CⲰN
MHIIANTEC
AIIOCTOⲖOI
MHIIANTEC
IIPOФHTAI

ⲀIKNYMIEANTA·
ⲅⲖⲰCCEⲖICⲦⲰNⲀ
ⲐPⲰIIⲰNⲀⲖⲖⲰⲔ
TⲰNAⲅⲅEⲖⲰNAⲅⲀ
IIHNⲀⲖEMHEXⲰ
OYⲐENEIMI
KAIEANⲧⲰMICⲰ
IIANTATAYIIAPX⁻
TAMOYKAIEANIIA
PAⲖⲰTOCⲰMAMⲓ
INAKAYXHCⲰMⲚ
AⲅAIIHNⲀⲖEMHE
XⲰOYⲐENⲰФ·Ⲭⲓ
MAI
HⲀⲅAIIH
MAKPOⲐYMEI
XPHCTEYETAI
HⲀⲅAIIH
OYZHⲖOI
HⲀⲅAIIH
OYIIEPIIEPEYETⲀⲓ
OYФYCIOYTAI
OYKACXHMONEI
OYZHTITAEAYTHC
OYIIAPOZYNETⲀⲓ
OYⲖOⲅIZETAITOKⲚ·
OYXAIPEIEIIITHⲀ
AIKIACYⲅXAIPIⲀ·
THAAHⲐIA
IIANTACTEⲅEI
IIANTAIIICTEYEI
IIANTAEⲖIIIZEI
IIANTAYIIOMENEI
HⲀⲅAIIHOYⲖEIIO

3. Detail of Codex Sinaiticus folio 272 showing the top of columns two and three with the text of 1 Corinthians 12:24–29 and 12:31 – 13:8.

4. Codex Alexandrinus folio 36 showing Luke 18:9–36.

5. Cursive manuscript 699 folio 135 showing John 5:33 – 6:1.

6. St Catherine's Monastery, Mount Sinai.

καὶ καταχθονίων, 11 καὶ πᾶσα γλῶσσα ἐξομολογήσεται ὅτι κύ-
ριοσ Ἰησοῦσ Χριστὸσ εἰσ δόξαν θεοῦ πατρόσ.

12 Ὥστε, ἀγαπητοί μου, καθὼσ πάντοτε ὑπηκούσατε, μὴ ὡσ
ἐν τῇ παρουσίᾳ μου μόνον ἀλλὰ νῦν πολλῷ μᾶλλον ἐν τῇ ἀπουσίᾳ Eph 6, 5
μου, μετὰ φόβου καὶ τρόμου τὴν ἑαυτῶν σωτηρίαν κατεργάζεσθε·
13 θεὸσ γάρ ἐστιν ὁ ἐνεργῶν ἐν ὑμῖν καὶ τὸ θέλειν καὶ τὸ ἐνεργεῖν
ὑπὲρ τῆσ εὐδοκίασ. 14 πάντα ποιεῖτε χωρὶσ γογγυσμῶν καὶ δια- 1 Pe 4, 9
λογισμῶν, 15 ἵνα γένησθε ἄμεμπτοι καὶ ἀκέραιοι, τέκνα θεοῦ
ἄμωμα μέσον γενεᾶσ σκολιᾶσ καὶ διεστραμμένησ, ἐν οἷσ φαίνεσθε

---

⁴¹⁷ et Thdotclem ²⁶⁹ Or³,⁸⁴⁹ et⁴,¹⁴⁴ etcat luc ᴺᵈ Euspraep⁷⁴ Ath³⁵⁰ Euthal
cod Chr²⁵¹· ²⁸⁷ Cyrioh⁹⁵⁰ etfid ¹⁰ᵏ Thdrt etc ... P al aliq (3 ap Scri)
ινα - καμψει. Huc non valent tot patrum loci ubi verba apostoli mu-
tata oratione afferuntur, ut Or¹,²⁶ᴹ καὶ ὁρῶντι ὅτι ἐν τῷ - κάμψει,
Eusps⁰⁴³ ὅτι πᾶν - κάμψει etc.

11. ἐξομολογήσεται cum ACDEFGKLP al plus³⁵ Or²,⁵⁴⁹ et⁴,¹⁴⁴ etcat luc⁸⁶
Ath³⁵⁰ cdd ⁸ Chr²⁸⁸ Euthalcod (rursus ea tantum testimonia huc valent
quae etiam ινα etc continent) ... ς Ln (errans circa D) ἐξομολογήση-
ται cum ℵB al plu Ir⁴⁸ Clem⁴¹⁷ et Thdotclem ¹⁶⁰ Euspraep⁷⁴ Ath³⁵⁰ed
Chr²⁸¹ Cyrioh⁹⁵⁰ etfid ¹⁰⁸ Thdrt | οτι κυριοσ ιησουσ χριστοσ et. Clem
⁴¹⁷ Or¹,⁷⁸⁶· ²,⁵⁴⁹ et³,²⁴²· ⁴,¹⁴⁴ etcat luc ᴺᵈ etint³,⁹⁶¹ Eusecl²⁷· ⁷⁴ etesa 149
Ath³⁵⁰ Cyrioh⁹⁵⁹ etc Cyp²⁹⁰· ³¹⁷ Ambrst al ... FᵍℂG g m⁵ Orint¹,⁵⁸ Eus
ps⁶⁴³ Didtri³⁶³ Novat³⁰⁵ (Gall⁸) Hil¹⁷⁷· ¹⁸⁹· ³²⁴ acsaep οτι κυρ. ιησουσ
(omisso χρι.) ... κ οτι χριστοσ κυριοσ, Thdotclem⁹⁶⁹ libere οτι κυριοσ
τησ δοξησ ιησ. χριστ. σωτηρ, Victorin quod Iesus Chri. dominus noster

12. αγαπητοι: A lectionaria aliq demid addidit αδελφοι | ωσ et. it vg (et. am
fu demid etc) syrP: B 3. 17. 38. 48. 72. 178. hal harl** syrsch cop
arm aeth Chr²⁹⁴cod Ambrst al om | εν τη παρουσια: ℵᶜFᵍℂG d e g fu
allachm om εν | νυν: DEFG d e f g vg arm Victorin Ambrst al post
πολλ. μαλλον pon ... 4. 33. 115. Chrᶜᵒᵐ²⁰⁴ Thphyl om | εν τη απου-
σια μου: FᵍℂG g om (f sub ÷ habet)

13. θεοσ sine articulo cum ℵABCD*FGKP 17. al pauc Eusluc (ap Mai¹⁰²)
Euthalcod Dam ... ς (Gbᵐᵐ) praem ο cum DᵇᵉᵗᶜEL al pler Chr Thdrt
al | ενεργων: 17. post εν υμιν pon ... A add δυναμεισ | ευδοκιασ: C
aeth add αυτου

14. και διαλογισμων: K 43. 71. om

15. γενησθε cum ℵBCDᶜEᵉᵉKLP al omnvi Chr Euthalcod Philcarp⁷³⁴
(Gall⁹) Cyrthes ²⁸⁴ Thdrt Antioch¹⁰⁷⁶ Dam al ... Lu ητε cum AD*E*
FG it vg Cyp³⁰⁹ Orint²,³²³ Victorin Ambrst al | αμεμπτ. κ. ακερ.: 17.
ακερ. κ. αμ. | αμωμα cum ℵABC 17. 23. Clem³¹⁰ Victoringraece (- non
eritis maculati, inquit Latinus. Graecus tamen ita posuit: αμωμα τεκνα,
id est filii sine vituperatione.) Cyrthes²⁸⁴ ... ς Ti αμωμητα cum DEFG
KLP al pler Chr²⁹⁴ Philcarp Euthalcod Thdrt Dam al | μεσον (Gb'')
cum ℵABCD*FGP 17. 23. 31. 67** 73. Clem Euthalcod ... ς εν μεσω

---

7. Page 713 of the 8th edition of Tischendorf's Greek New Testament.

40 ⁴⁰ Καὶ ἔρχεται πρὸς αὐτὸν λεπρὸς παρακαλῶν αὐτὸν καὶ γονυπετῶν ;καὶ; λέγων
41 αὐτῷ. ὅτι, ἐὰν θέλῃς. δύνασαί με καθαρίσαι. ⁴¹ ὁ δὲ Ἰησοῦς σπλαγχνισθεὶς ἐκτεί-
42 νας τὴν χεῖρα αὐτοῦ ἥψατο καὶ λέγει αὐτῷ· θέλω. καθαρίσθητι. ⁴² καὶ εἰπόντος
43 αὐτοῦ εὐθὺς ἀπῆλθεν ἀπ᾽ αὐτοῦ ἡ λέπρα. καὶ ἐκαθαρίσθη. ⁴³ καὶ ἐμβριμησάμενος
44 αὐτῷ εὐθὺς ἐξέβαλεν αὐτὸν ⁴⁴ καὶ λέγει αὐτῷ· ὅρα μηδενὶ μηδὲν εἴπῃς. ἀλλὰ ὕπαγε
σεαυτὸν δεῖξον τῷ ἱερεῖ καὶ προσένεγκε περὶ τοῦ καθαρισμοῦ σου. ἃ προσέταξεν
45 Μωϋσῆς. εἰς μαρτύριον αὐτοῖς. ⁴⁵ ὁ δὲ ἐξελθὼν ἤρξατο κηρύσσειν πολλὰ καὶ
διαφημίζειν τὸν λόγον. ὥστε μηκέτι αὐτὸν δύνασθαι εἰς πόλιν φανερῶς εἰσελθεῖν.
ἀλλ᾽ ἔξω ἐπ᾽ ἐρήμοις τόποις ἦν. καὶ ἤρχοντο πρὸς αὐτὸν πάντοθεν.

40 om και Mt 8₂ Lk 5₁₂ //δ¹ ²· δω /ᶜ⁰ᵇ˙⁴⁵· af η   41 . ηφατο αυτου (Mt 8₃ Lk 5₁₃)
K gg //δ¹·²·⁵⁶·¹⁰¹⁶ /ᶜ²⁸⁶·³⁵⁰¹ Kʳ. αυτου bi· Ta /ᶜδ⁵· η ᵇ²¹¹ ·¹³⁴¹ pa lat ;αυτου · αυτου
bc) sy ᶜ (1442)

40 add αυτον p γονυπετων Ta K gg // ᵈ⁵ δ¹ δ¹⁸ ⁷⁶ ᴋᵃ /ᶜ⁹³ ˛ ᵉˣᶜᵇ²⁰³¹ η ·ᵉˣᶜ δ³⁰ ᵇ¹³³³ ·²⁵⁴·¹²⁸⁴
gᵃ¹²¹ᶠᵇ¹⁰⁴³·³⁷¹ arm. add αυτω /ᵈ⁵ η ᵇ³⁶⁰·δ³⁶²·ᵤ¹²⁷⁹·ᵣ¹⁰²⁰·¹⁴⁴³. om και γονυπ. (αυτον · αυτον)
;Mt 8₂; //δ¹ /ᵈ⁵ rᵇ¹²¹¹ η ·¹²¹⁶·³⁰⁰·ᵢ⁴¹²¹·α³⁵¹·ₓ₋¹⁰⁹⁹· ⁵⁰·²⁴³·³⁷⁰·¹⁴¹⁶ K¹⁸⁷ abc rᶠ ff² add
κυριε a οτι ;Mt 8₂ Lk 5₁₂; //δ¹·δ³·⁵⁶·¹⁰¹⁶ /ᵈ⁰¹⁴¹ ˛ᵣ¹⁸ pa af ˛ arm. add p θελης //δ³⁷¹ /ᵃ⁹³ᶠ
ᵣᵇ¹²¹¹ ᵤ¹²⁷⁹ ᵣᵢ⁷ α³⁵¹ ˸ om οτι (Mt 8₂) //δ³·⁵⁶·³⁷⁶ /ᵈδ⁵ᶠ ˛ᵣ¹⁸ lat ᵉˣᶜᵈ arm   41 και 1 o
δε ἰς ;Mt 8₃ Lk 5₁₃; //δ¹·²·¹⁰¹⁶ ᵇ⁷ /ᵈ⁸⁵ af it. ˛ σπλαγχ. δε o ἰς //³⁴⁶ η | οργισθεις 1 σπλαγχνι-
σθεις Ta ˛ /ᵈ⁸⁵ α ff² r. om σπλαγχ. b   λεγων | και λεγει (ᵤₒ) /ᵃ⁰¹⁴·⁹³ ˛ ²²⁶ και λεγων | om
αυτω ;Mt 8₃ nö) //δ² /ᵃ⁰¹⁴ ˛ ᵉˣᶜᵇ³⁰¹⁵·δ³⁶·ᵤₒᵢ·¹⁰⁵⁴ ˛ ff² syP   42 om ειποντος αυτου (Mt 8₃
Lk 5₁₃) Ta H ᵉˣᶜ δ³·δ⁴ᴺ·⁷⁶·³⁷⁶¹ /ᵈδ⁵·⁹³ ˛ᵉˣᶜᵃᵇ¹²¹¹·²²⁶ η ᵇ³⁶⁰· af it syᶜᵉ   ευθεως K gg
//δ¹·²·δ⁴ᴺ /ᵈ⁰⁵⁰ ˛ η λεπρα a απηλθεν (Lk 5₁₃) //δ¹·¹⁰¹⁶ᶠᶠ /η ᵇ³⁶⁰· 1493 ˛ η λεπρα απ
αυτου H⁷⁶ ˛ om σπ) /ᵃ⁹³·₃³⁰¹⁷ η ·¹¹³·²¹¹·¹³³³ /ₐ¹²⁹ᶠᶠ·¹²⁷⁹ om σπ·²⁷⁰·πₓ ·²⁹ K¹⁹⁴ ff² syh
εκαθαρ— //ᵉˣᶜδ¹ᶜ·²·δ⁴ᴺ·¹⁰¹⁶ /ᵈ⁹³·₀·δ²⁵⁴·δ⁴⁵⁷·η²¹¹·ᵢᵖ¹⁰⁴³·¹⁸·ₓ·δ¹·⁷³⁰·²⁹·⁹⁵·²⁴³·¹³⁵⁴ K¹⁶¹
¹⁰²⁷·¹⁷⁷·   43 ευθεως K gg //ᵉˣᶜδ³·⁷⁶·δ³⁷¹ /ᵈ⁸⁵ ˛ 1341. om ευθυς (cᶠ Lk 5₁₄) /ᵉᶜ²¹⁹ φᵇ¹³³³
gᵇ¹⁴³⁵ ˛²⁴⁷·¹³⁵³ syᵉᶜᵐᵉ   44 om μηδεν /ᵞᵃ³⁰¹⁵· ⁹⁵. om μηδεν //δ¹·δ⁴ᴺ Lk 5₁₄) H ᵉˣᶜδ¹·
δ³·³⁷⁶ /ᵃδ⁵ᶠ·¹³³·⁹³ ˛η ᵃᵇ¹²¹⁶·³⁰¹⁵ ᵐᵍᵈᵉˣ¹ ᵐᵍᵈᵉˣⁿ ᵉ¹⁰⁸¹ᶠ·¹⁰⁹⁴ʲᵖₓ·⁸⁴ ᵣ¹³⁴¹·1385·1416·1493 lat
αλλ K⁰ Kʳ (1377f)   45 ˛ φανερως εις πολιν K gg //ᵉˣᶜ δ³·⁷⁶·³⁷⁶¹ /ᵃ⁹³ᶠ·ᵣᵇ¹²¹¹·ᵢ ₒ¹²⁷⁹ ᵢ
1416. ˛ φανερως εισελθ. εις π. /ᵈδ⁵ ff² syᶜᵉᵉ   ev 1 εκ ;Lk 5₁₄ 9₁₂; K gg //ᵉˣᶜδ³·δ⁴⁸·³⁷⁶ᶠ /ᵈ
⁰¹⁴·⁹³ᶠ·ᵣᵇ¹²¹¹·   πανταχοθεν Kˣ Kʳ gg H ˛/ᵃδ⁵ᶠ·⁹³ ˛·η αᵇ¹⁰⁸⁶·ᵣ⁷²·ₒ¹²⁷⁹·²⁷⁰·πₓ·ₒ¹¹³²·ₓᵉˣᶜ
ᶜ²⁹⁴·³²⁹⁰·²⁹·¹²⁴⁶·³⁷⁰¹·¹³⁵⁴·¹³⁸⁶¹ K¹⁶¹·⁹⁴·¹⁷⁷·¹⁰²⁷ (1442)

40 ερωτων | παρ. /ᵃδ⁵· | om αυτον /ᵃᵉ·δ⁴⁵·²⁵⁷·²¹⁹·   om αυτω ;Mt 8₂; //³⁷⁶ /ᵃδ⁵ᶠ·¹³³·ᵢ⁰¹³⁴⁹·ₒ⁵⁵¹·
⁷⁰·¹⁴¹⁶·¹⁴⁴³ itᵉˣᶜ/ vg ˛ θελησης /ᵃδ⁵¹ δυνη //δ¹   41 add και a εκτεινας /¹³⁸⁶/ᵉₚ add και p χειρα
/²⁴³ᵃ 42. ευθ. a ειπ. /¹¹⁴³. om ευθυς bc add ευθεως του λογου ειποντος a και εκαθ. /φᵃ⁴¹³. add
απ αυτου p εκαθ. /ᵉᶜ²²⁶ om και εκαθαρισθη /ᵃ⁰¹¹ af b   43 om a ˛⁻) /ᵃ⁰¹⁴ bc ˛ om και /φ
ᵇ³⁰¹⁵· om εμβριμ.— ευθυς af ˛ ενεβριμσαμενος /ᵃδ⁵·⁰⁵⁰· om αυτω /η ᵃ¹⁶⁷·¹¹³˸·¹²⁴⁶·ₐ. αυτου 1
αυτω /¹³⁸⁶ ˸ add p αυτ. /ᵃᵉˣᶜ·δ²⁹¹·³²⁹. om εξεβ. αυτ. syᵉᶜ 44 ειπων 1 και λεγει /ᵃ¹³³·
⁹³. ειπεν 1 λεγει /ᵃ¹⁸⁸ᴺ ᵤ ᵣ f ˛ δειξ. σεαυτου /ᵃδ⁵¹·⁰¹¹ᵉᵃᵛ⁻ lat αρχιερει //δ⁴⁸·¹⁰¹⁶ᵐ /ᵃᵉˣᶜ
ᵇ¹⁰³³¹ᵍᵇ¹⁴³⁵ vg ˛ προσενεγκαι //δ³·⁵⁶ /ᵃᵈ⁵⁰·η·δ³⁰ᶠ·ᵤ¹²⁹¹·ₓ·δ⁴⁷⁰·²⁹ Kʳ.–κον /ᵃ⁹³ (1367)
υπερ | περι //δ⁴⁸ᴺ add αυτου p περι /¹¹⁸ ˛ οια (Mt 8₄) //³⁷⁶ /ᵃ⁰¹⁴¹¹ q·δ³⁰ᶠ·
¹³⁸⁶·ᵤᶜ. καθως //δ³⁰ syᵉᶜ. καθα //δ⁴ᴺ Μωσης Kˣ Kʳ (1374) αυτω | αυτοις /ₓ·δ¹ᵉᵛ   45 om
πολλα /ᵃδ⁵ᶠ lat add αυτου p λογου /η ᶜ¹⁰⁸⁶¹ ˛ αυτ. μηκ. /¹¹¹⁶. om μηκετι //³⁷⁶. ˛ δυνασθαι
αυτ. //δ² /ᵃ¹³³ ᵤ·⁴¹³·ₒ¹²⁷⁹·ᵣᵢ⁷·ₒ¹²²⁶. om αυτου /ᵃδ⁵¹ ˛ ελθ. 1 εισελθ. /²⁴⁷·¹²⁴⁶·¹⁴⁴³ ˛ αλλα
//δ³·⁷⁶ /ᵃδ⁵·φᵇ¹⁰⁸⁶·⁷²·ₒ¹²²²·ₓ·δ⁴·³²⁹·δ²⁶⁰·¹³⁸⁶· om ην //δ¹ af b om πανταθεν af b add
και ελαλει αυτοις τον λογον p παντ.·²₂) //³⁷⁶ ˛

8. Page 124 of von Soden's Greek New Testament.

8: 5-7

5. Ἐξῆλθεν ὁ σπείρων τοῦ σπεῖραι τὸν σπόρον αὐτοῦ· καὶ ἐν τῷ σπείρειν αὐτὸν ὃ μὲν ἔπεσε παρὰ τὴν ὁδόν, καὶ κατεπατήθη, καὶ τὰ πετεινὰ τοῦ οὐρανοῦ κατέφαγεν αὐτό· (= Mt 13: 3-4/Mk 4: 4)

INDEX LECTT: 8: 5-15 inc. I εξηλθεν (τη κυρ της δ) l524   inc. VI εξηλθεν (τη κυρ της δ) l12 l32 l48 l70 l150 l184 l211 l253 l292 l299 l547 l854 l859 l890 l950 l1016 l1056 l1074 l1231 l1627 l1634 l1663 l1761   8: 5-15 + 20: 21-25 inc. VI   εξηλθεν (τη κυρ της δ) LECT l80 l1127 l1579 l1642

DEF: p⁷⁵ frag (εξη|)πειραι τον |]ω σπειφ|]ν αυτον . . . αυτα) C P R (inc. σπορον) 0135 0202 0267 1194 1220

PATR: εξηλθεν . . . αυτου Cat Mk (Cramer, Catenae 305): Ath exp Pss 106. 37 (PG 27. 452); εξηλθεν . . . σπειραι ‡sem 2 (PG 28. 145): (5-8) εξηλθεν . . . αυτου Chrys ‡hom in Ps 77-107 Ps 106 (PG 55. 671); (5, 7, 6) εξηλθεν . . . σπειραι bis ‡hom in Lc (PG 61. 773f): εξηλθεν . . . αυτου Cyr hom pasch 2. 7 (PG 77. 444); εξηλθεν . . . αυτου bis Is 5. 2 (PG 70. 1197 et 1233f); Os-Mal (Pusey 2. 135); τα πετεινα του ουρανου fr Mt (TU 61. 207): εξηλθεν . . . σπειραι Diod Ps 88: 36 (PG 33. 1622): Eus Ps 88 (PG 23. 1108); Is 53 (PG 24. 460): (5, 8) Hipp haer 8. 9. 1 (GCS 26. 227): εξηλθεν . . . σπειραι Or comm in Pr (PG 13. 25); comm in Cor 41 (JTS 9. 511): εξηλθεν . . . αυτου TitBost fr Lc (TU 21. 1. 173)   LATT εξηλθεν . . . οδον AM Ps 36, 12, 2 (CSEL 64. 78): AN Mt h 25 (PG 56. 761): εξηλθεν EUCH int 3 (CSEL 31. 15): ORI ser 9 (GCS 38. 15) ADAPT PS-AU s Gue 3, 1 (PLS 2. 132)   SYRR εξηλθεν . . . οδον Ephr Comm 11, 12 (Leloir 62 cp. CSCO 137. 149)

εξηλθεν: [ιδου εξηλθεν] Lvt (e a aur b ff² g¹ gat l q r¹) Ss Sc AM Ephr; 'the lord spoke this parable behold' Sj; [ιδου] Cb (1 ms.)   του σπειραι: om. A*
του¹: om. D K W Π 0211 472 489 565 1009 1012 1079 1219 1229 1313 1355 1604 2487 Cat Mk Cyr hom pasch   σπειραι . . . τω: om. 716   σπειραι: σπειμειν 2643 l524   του . . . αυτου: om. Lvt (c) Ss Sc   σπερμα Cat Mk   σπορου αυτου: ιδιου σπορου TitBost   σπορου: λογον 700; |αγρου] Lvt (l) AM   αυτου: εαυτου A G M V Γ Δ Ω 0208 0211 16 22 28 123 161 179 230ᶜ 262 348 399 461 475 477 478 543 669* 713 826 828 1005 1080 1192 1195 1216ᶜ 1223 1242* 1295 1351 1352 1365 1452 1579 1604 1691 2372 l48 l292; αυτων 131 1187*; om.

D Et (Bodl. 40) Just   και¹ . . . οδου: om. AM
και¹ . . . επεσε: om. Lvt (a)   και¹: + εγενετο l890
σπειρεω: σπειραι 1319   αυτου: om. D Lvt Lvg Go OS (mss.)   ο μεν: om. Go   ο: α B W 2643 Cs; +
γαρ 66ᶜ   μεν: om. Lvt (e a aur b c f ff² g¹ gat l q r¹)
Lvg   παρα: επι R 443 Et   και κατεπατηθη: om.
Dtp   και²: om. 700 Cs (1 ms.)   κατεπατηθη: + υπο των ανθρωπων 472 1009; [κατεπατησαν αυτο] Lvt (g¹)
και³ . . . αυτο: om. Lvt (g¹)   του ουρανου: om. D W
Lvt (e a b d ff² l q) Ss Sc Sp Dta Dtp   κατεφαγεν
αυτο: 2, 1 Lvt (b ff² l q)   κατεφαγεν: κατεφαγον Θᶜ
21 1219 l1074; εφαγεν 1654   αυτο: αυτα p⁷⁵ B 16 21 1012 1604 Cs

6. καὶ ἕτερον ἔπεσεν ἐπὶ τὴν πέτραν, καὶ φυὲν ἐξηράνθη διὰ τὸ μὴ ἔχειν ἰκμάδα·

DEF: C F (expl. επεσεν) P 0135 0202 0267 1194 1220

PATR: ADAPT (5-8) Chrys ‡hom in Ps 77-107 Ps 106 (PG 55. 671); (5, 7, 6) ‡hom in Lc (PG 61. 774): Cyr Jo 4. 4 (Pusey 3. 575)   LATT και¹ . . . πετραν AM Ps 36, 12, 2 (CSEL 64. 78): AN Mt h 25 (PG 56. 761)   SYRR ADAPT Ephr Comm 11, 12 (Leloir 62 cp. CSCO 137. 149)

και ετερον: [ετερον δε] Cb (6 mss.)   και¹: om. Cs (2 mss.) Cb (1 ms.) AM AN   ετερον: ετερος 700; αλλο D Cb; [ετερα] Cs   επεσεν: κατεπεσεν p⁷⁵ B L R Ξ 700 l890; om. Lvt (e) AM AN   επι: εις 827; παρα Ξ 131 349 1071   την πετραν: 'a place of rock' Cb (2 mss.); 'the places of rock' Cs (1 ms.); [τα πετρωδη] Lvt (gat)

την: om. p⁷⁵ B 579 2766* Cb   πετραν: + οπου ουκ ειχε γην πολλην 1604; [γην] Lvt (b)   και³: om. Gg (II. III)   φυεν: φυεις 700; εφυεν L l1074 Cb (mss.); + [και] Gg   εξηρανθη: + και S*   ικμαδα: ριζαν 579 Et

9. Detail from page 165 of the International Greek New Testament Project's apparatus to Luke's Gospel.

ἐπὶ μῆνας τρεῖς διαλεγόμενος καὶ πείθων °[τὰ] περὶ τῆς βασιλείας· τοῦ θεοῦ. 9 ⌜ὡς δέ τινες⌝ ἐσκληρύνοντο καὶ ἠπείθουν κακολογοῦντες τὴν ὁδὸν ἐνώπιον τοῦ πλήθους ᵀ, ἀποστὰς ἀπ' αὐτῶν ἀφώρισεν τοὺς μαθητὰς καθ' ἡμέραν διαλεγόμενος ἐν τῇ σχολῇ Τυράννου ᵀ. 10 τοῦτο δὲ ἐγένετο ἐπὶ ἔτη δύο, ⌜ὥστε πάντας τοὺς κατοικοῦντας τὴν Ἀσίαν ἀκοῦσαι τὸν λόγον τοῦ κυρίου, Ἰουδαίους τε καὶ Ἕλληνας⌝. · 11 Δυνάμεις τε οὐ τὰς τυχούσας ὁ θεὸς ἐποίει διὰ τῶν χειρῶν Παύλου, 12 ὥστε καὶ ἐπὶ τοὺς ἀσθενοῦντας ἀποφέρεσθαι ἀπὸ τοῦ χρωτὸς °αὐτοῦ σουδάρια ἢ σιμικίνθια καὶ ἀπαλλάσσεσθαι °¹ἀπ' αὐτῶν τὰς νόσους, τά τε πνεύματα τὰ πονηρὰ ἐκπορεύεσθαι.

13 Ἐπεχείρησαν δέ τινες καὶ τῶν περιερχομένων Ἰουδαίων ἐξορκιστῶν ὀνομάζειν ἐπὶ τοὺς ἔχοντας τὰ πνεύματα τὰ πονηρὰ τὸ ὄνομα τοῦ κυρίου Ἰησοῦ λέγοντες· ⌜ὁρκίζω ὑμᾶς τὸν Ἰησοῦν ὃν Παῦλος κηρύσσει. 14 ⌜ἦσαν δέ ⌜τινος Σκευᾶ Ἰουδαίου ἀρχιερέως ἑπτὰ υἱοὶ ᵀ τοῦτο ποιοῦντες.⌝ 15 ⌜ἀποκριθὲν δὲ⌝ τὸ πνεῦμα τὸ πονηρὸν ᵀ εἶπεν αὐτοῖς· τὸν °[μὲν] Ἰησοῦν γινώσκω καὶ τὸν Παῦλον ἐπίσταμαι, ὑμεῖς δὲ τίνες ἐστέ; 16 καὶ ⌜ἐφαλόμενος ⌜ὁ ἄνθρωπος ἐπ' αὐτοὺς⌝ ἐν ᾧ ἦν τὸ πνεῦμα τὸ πονηρόν, ᶠκατακυριεύσας ⌐¹ἀμφοτέρων ἴσχυσεν κατ' αὐτῶν ὥστε γυμνοὺς καὶ τετραυματισμένους ἐκφυγεῖν ἐκ τοῦ οἴκου ἐκείνου. 17 τοῦτο δὲ ἐγένετο γνωστὸν πᾶσιν Ἰουδαίοις τε

Marginal references (right column):

17,17!
8,12; 20,25; 28,23. 31 L 4,43!
9,2!
2 K 6,17 R 16,17!
18,11; 20,31 1 K 16,8
1.22.26s; 6,9; 16,6; 20,4.16.18; 21,27! · 14,1! |
5,15 Mc 6,56p!
J 11,44!

L 9,49p
16,18

L 4,41p · 16,17

1,19! · 14,1!

---

8 °† B D Ψ 1175. 1891ᶜ pc ¦ txt ℵ A E 33. 1739 𝔐 • 9 ⌜τινες μεν ουν αυτων D | ᵀτων εθνων. Τοτε D (E) syph** | ᵀ τινος Ε Ψ 𝔐 vgᶜˡ (syp) ¦ τιν. απο ωρας ε΄ εως δεκατης D (614 pc) gig w syh** ¦ txt 𝔓⁷⁴ ℵ A B 323. 945. 1739 pc r vgˢˡ • 10 ⌜εως παντες οι κ-τες τ. Α. ηκουσαν τους λογους τ. κ., I-οι και E-νες D* (e syp) • 12 ° 𝔓³⁸ | °¹ 𝔓⁷⁴ pc • 13 ⌜-ζομεν 𝔐 ¦ εξορκιζομεν 𝔓³⁸ 36. 453. 614. 945. 1739. 1891 pc ¦ txt 𝔓⁷⁴ ℵ A B D E Ψ 33. 1175 pc samˢ bo • 14 ⌜εν οις και υι. (+ επτα syʰᵐᵍ) Σ. (+ Ιουδαιου 𝔓³⁸) τινος ιερεως (αρχιερ. 𝔓³⁸) ηθελησαν το αυτο ποιησαι. εθος ειχαν τους τοιουτους εξορκιζειν (εχοντες εξορ. τ. τοι. 𝔓³⁸)· και εισελθοντες προς τον (– 𝔓³⁸) δαιμονιζομενον ηρξαντο επικαλεισθαι το ονομα λεγοντες· παραγγελλομεν σοι εν Ιησου ον Παυλος (+ ο αποστολος 𝔓³⁸) κηρυσσει εξελθειν (εξ. κηρ. D*) 𝔓³⁸ D (w syʰᵐᵍ) ¦ ⌜τινες 𝔓⁷⁴ ℵ A Ψ 33 𝔐 lat syʰ ¦ txt 𝔓⁴¹ B D E 36. 453. 1175. 1739. 1891 pc p* syp ¦ ᵀοι Ε Ψ 𝔐 syh ¦ txt 𝔓⁴¹·⁷⁴ᵛⁱᵈ ℵ A B 33. 945. 1175. 1739. 1891 pc • 15 ⌜τοτε απεκριθη D ¦ ᵀκαι D¹ ¦ ° 𝔓³⁸ᵛⁱᵈ·⁷⁴ ℵ* A D 33. 1739 𝔐 latt co ¦ txt 𝔓⁴¹ ℵ² B E Ψ 614. 1505 pc syh • 16 ⌜εφαλλ- 𝔓⁴¹ ℵ² Ε Ψ 33. 1739 𝔐 ¦ εναλλ- D ¦ txt 𝔓⁷⁴ ℵ* A B 1175 pc ¦ ⌜3 4 1 2 𝔓⁷⁴ (D) 𝔐 ¦ 1 2 (E, sed pon. 3 4 p. πον.) 945. 1739. 1891 pc ¦ txt 𝔓⁴¹ ℵ A B Ψ 33. 36. 614. 1175. 1505 al | ⌜ και (– ℵ²) κατακ- ℵ* (Ψ) 104. 323. 453. 1241 al ¦ κ. (– A pc) κατακ-σαν A 𝔐 ¦ κυριευσας D pc ¦ κατεκ-σεν 1739. 1891 pc ¦ txt 𝔓⁷⁴ B E 33. 614. 1175. 1505 al | ⌐¹αυτων (Ψ) 1739 𝔐 ¦ – E ¦ txt 𝔓⁷⁴ ℵ A B D 33. 36. 104. 614. 1175. 1505 pc syh

10. Page 379 of the 27th edition of the Nestle-Aland Greek New Testament.

αὐτῷ ὁ Ἰησοῦς, Πορεύου, ὁ υἱός σου ζῇ.ᶜᶜ ἐπίστευσεν ὁ
ἄνθρωπος τῷ λόγῳ ὃν εἶπεν αὐτῷ ὁ Ἰησοῦς καὶ ἐπορεύετο.
51 ἤδη δὲ αὐτοῦ καταβαίνοντος οἱ δοῦλοι αὐτοῦ ὑπήντη-
σαν αὐτῷ λέγοντες ὅτι ὁ παῖς αὐτοῦ[7] ζῇ.ᵈᵈ **52** ἐπύθετο
οὖν τὴν ὥραν παρ᾽ αὐτῶν ἐν ᾗ κομψότερον ἔσχεν· εἶπαν
οὖν αὐτῷ ὅτι Ἐχθὲς ὥραν ἑβδόμην ἀφῆκεν αὐτὸν ὁ
πυρετός.ᵉᶜ **53** ἔγνω οὖν ὁ πατὴρ ὅτι [ἐν] ἐκείνῃ τῇ ὥρᾳ ἐν
ᾗ εἶπεν αὐτῷ ὁ Ἰησοῦς, Ὁ υἱός σου ζῇ, καὶ ἐπίστευσεν
αὐτὸς καὶ ἡ οἰκία αὐτοῦ ὅλη.ᶠᶠ **54** Τοῦτο [δὲ] πάλιν
δεύτερον σημεῖον ἐποίησεν ὁ Ἰησοῦς ἐλθὼν ἐκ τῆς
Ἰουδαίας εἰς τὴν Γαλιλαίαν.ᵍᵍ

The Healing at the Pool

5 Μετὰ ταῦτα ἦν ἑορτὴ[1] τῶν Ἰουδαίων καὶ ἀνέβη
Ἰησοῦς εἰς Ἱεροσόλυμα.ᵃ **2** ἔστιν δὲ ἐν τοῖς Ἱεροσολύμοις
ἐπὶ τῇ προβατικῇ κολυμβήθρα ἡ ἐπιλεγομένη Ἑβραϊστὶ
Βηθζαθὰ[2] πέντε στοὰς ἔχουσα. **3** ἐν ταύταις κατέκειτο

[7] **51** {B} παῖς αὐτοῦ 𝔓⁶⁶*. ⁷⁵ ℵ A B C Wˢᵘᵖᵖ / 1016 arm ‖ υἱός αὐτοῦ itᵃᵘʳ. ᶜ. ᵈ. ᶠ.
ᶠᶠ². ˡ. ʳ¹ vg Augustineᵛⁱᵈ ‖ παῖς σου Δ Θ Ψ 0233 f¹ 28 157 180 205 565 597 700 1006
1010 1243 1292 1342 1424 1505 Byz [E F G H] Lect syrʰ geo Heracleonᵃᶜᶜ. ᵗᵒ Origen
Origen Chrysostom ‖ υἱός σου 𝔓⁶⁶ᶜ D L N 0141 33 579 892 1071 1241 / 68 / 211 / 387
/ 547 / 672 (itᵃ. ᵇ. ᵉ. q) syrᶜ. ᵖ. ʰᵐᵍ. ᵖᵃˡ eth slav Cyrillᵉᵐ ‖ παῖς σου ὁ υἱός αὐτοῦ f¹³

[1] **1** {A} ἑορτή 𝔓⁶⁶. ⁷⁵ A B D T Wˢᵘᵖᵖ Θ f¹³ 28 180 565 579 700 1006 1241 1292
1505 Byzᵖᵗ [G N] arm geo Origen Epiphanius Chrysostom ‖ ἡ ἑορτή ℵ C L Δ Ψ 0141
0233ᵛⁱᵈ f¹ 33 157 205 597 828ᶜ 892 1010 1071 1243 1342 1424 Byzᵖᵗ [E F H] Amphilochius Cyrillᵉᵐ

[2] **2** {C} Βηθζαθά ℵ (L itᵉ Βηζαθά) 33 itˡ (itᵇ. ᶠᶠ²* vgᵐˢˢ Bet(h)zet(h)a) (Eusebius)
(Cyril) ‖ Βελζεθά D itᵈ. ʳ¹ (itᵃ Belzatha) ‖ Βηθσαιδά (see 1.44) (𝔓⁶⁶ᶜ Βηθσαιδά, 𝔓⁶⁶*
Βηθσαιδάν) 𝔓⁷⁵ B T Wˢᵘᵖᵖ (Ψ Βησσαιδά) itᵃᵘʳ. ᶜ. ᶠᶠ²ᶜ vg syrʰ copˢᵃ. ᵖᵇᵒ. ᵇᵒ. ᵃᶜʰ² eth Tertullian Chromatius Jerome ‖ Βηθεσδά A C Δ Θ 078 0141 0233 f¹ f¹³ 28 33 157 180 205
565 579 597 700 892 1006 1010 1071 1241 1243 1292 1342 (1424) 1505 Byz [E F G
H (N)] Lect itᶠ. q vgᵐˢˢ syrᶜ. ᵖ. ʰᵐᵍ ᵍʳ. ᵖᵃˡ arm geo slav Amphilochius Didymusᵈᵘᵇ Chrysostom Cyrillᵉᵐ

ᶜᶜ **50** SP: NA ‖ P: TEV FC NIV VP ᵈᵈ**51** P: TEV FC VP ᵉᶜ**52** P: FC NIV VP ᶠᶠ**53** P: TEV Seg FC
NIV VP NJB REB ᵍᵍ**54** P: AD NA M ‖ MS: WH NJB
ᵃ**5.1** P: NA RSV Seg NRSV

50 Πορεύου ... ζῇ Mt 8.13; Mk 7.29 **53** ἐπίστευσεν ... ὅλη Ac 11.14; 16.14-15. 31 **54** Jn 2.11

11. Page 329 of the United Bible Societies' *Greek New Testament.*

εἰς τὰ ἄμετρα καυχώμενοι ἐν ἀλλοτρίοις κόποις, ἐλπίδα δὲ ἔχοντες, αὐξανομένης τῆς πίστεως ὑμῶν, ἐν ὑμῖν μεγαλυνθῆναι κατὰ τὸν κανόνα ἡμῶν εἰς περισσείαν, **16** εἰς τὰ ὑπερέκεινα ὑμῶν εὐαγγελίσασθαι, οὐκ ἐν ἀλλοτρίῳ κανόνι εἰς τὰ ἕτοιμα καυχήσασθαι. **17** «Ὁ δὲ καυχώμενος, ἐν Κυρίῳ καυχάσθω.» **18** Οὐ γὰρ ὁ ἑαυτὸν ʳσυνιστῶν, ἐκεῖνός ἐστι δόκιμος, ἀλλ᾽ ὃν ὁ Κύριος συνίστησιν.

Paul's Concern for Believers' Fidelity

11 Ὄφελον ἀνείχεσθέ μου μικρὸν ʳτῇ ἀφροσύνῃʰ· ἀλλὰ καὶ ἀνέχεσθέ μου. **2** Ζηλῶ γὰρ ὑμᾶς Θεοῦ ζήλῳ,¹ ἡρμοσάμην γὰρ ὑμᾶς ἑνὶ ἀνδρὶ παρθένον ἁγνὴν παραστῆσαι τῷ Χριστῷ. **3** Φοβοῦμαι δὲ μή πως ὡς ὁ ὄφις ʳΕὕαν ἐξηπάτησενʰ ἐν τῇ πανουργίᾳ αὐτοῦ,ᵒοὕτω φθαρῇ τὰ νοήματα ὑμῶν ἀπὸ τῆς ἁπλότητος ᵀ τῆς εἰς τὸν Χριστόν. **4** Εἰ μὲν γὰρ ὁ ἐρχόμενος ἄλλον Ἰησοῦν κηρύσσει ὃν οὐκ ἐκηρύξαμεν, ἢ πνεῦμα ἕτερον λαμβάνετε ὃ οὐκ ἐλάβετε, ἢ εὐαγγέλιον ἕτερον ὃ οὐκ ἐδέξασθε, καλῶς ἀνείχεσθε.²

Paul Contrasted with False Apostles

5 Λογίζομαι γὰρ μηδὲν ὑστερηκέναι τῶν ὑπερλίαν ἀποστόλων. **6** Εἰ δὲ καὶ ἰδιώτης τῷ λόγῳ, ἀλλ᾽ οὐ τῇ γνώσει, ἀλλ᾽ ἐν παντὶ ʳφανερωθέντες ἐν πᾶσιν εἰς ὑμᾶς. **7** Ἢ ἁμαρτίαν ἐποίησα ἐμαυτὸν ταπεινῶν ἵνα ὑμεῖς ὑψωθῆτε, ὅτι δωρεὰν τὸ τοῦ Θεοῦ εὐαγγέλιον εὐηγγελισάμην ὑμῖν? **8** Ἄλλας ἐκκλησίας ἐσύλησα λαβὼν ὀψώνιον πρὸς τὴν ὑμῶν διακονίαν, **9** καὶ παρὼν πρὸς ὑμᾶς καὶ ὑστερηθείς, οὐ κατενάρκησα •οὐδενός· τὸ γὰρ

---

¹2 Θεου ζηλω **MʙB**, **TR Cr** vs ζηλω Θεου **Mᶜ**
²4 ανειχεσθε **Mᵖᵗℵ** vs ηνειχεσθε **Mᵖᵗ**, **TR** vs ανεχεσθε ⅌⁴⁶**B, Cr**

18 ʳσυνιστανων ⅌⁴⁶ℵ**B** vs **M**   1 ʳτι αφροσυνης ⅌⁴⁶ᵛⁱᵈℵ**B** vs 𝔐
3 ʳℵ**B** vs 𝔐   3 ᵒ⅌⁴⁶ℵ**B** vs 𝔐
3 ᵀκαι της αγνοτητος ⅌⁴⁶ℵ*B, [Cr] vs 𝔐
6 ʳφανερωσαντες ℵ*B vs 𝔐; (− αλλ εν παντι το υμας ⅌⁴⁶)
9 •ουθενος ℵB vs 𝔐⅌⁴⁶

---

17 Jer. 9:24

12. Page 563 of Hodges and Farstad's edition of the Majority Text.

quoting the NT from memory, or he may have adapted the text deliberately for his own purposes, or the Father's text may have been conformed to a prevailing later standard by copyists of the patristic work. But there are occasions when, after sufficient safeguards have been put in place and one is reasonably confident that the Father was citing a manuscript, his testimony may properly be included in an apparatus. In the past, apparatuses have been overloaded with the mere names of Fathers. Modern editors are trying to be more selective and informative when adding patristic testimony – but we still have some way to go before we should accept blindly that just because a patristic reference appears in an apparatus it really supports the reading in question.

Families

It is a matter of much interest that only a very small proportion of the large number of extant manuscripts can be shown to be copies of ones that we already know. Manuscripts are all individuals and must be largely treated as such. Obviously, all our Greek manuscripts have been copied from others. Only rarely have a manuscript and a copy taken from it both survived. Our 5,000 or so manuscripts represent only the tip of a very large iceberg of all the manuscripts ever written. Most manuscripts have disappeared. That means there are innumerable gaps. Despite hopeful suggestions by an older generation of scholars, it has proved impossible to draw up a genealogy of manuscripts and work back to a supposed original. Apart from huge gaps, there has been too much 'cross-fertilization' and 'intermarriage' between manuscripts to enable us to trace family relationships on a large scale.

In a very limited way some family relationships within NT manuscripts have, however, been identified. These are recognized because of certain common mistakes or shared readings. One such family, comprising cursive number 1 and perhaps a dozen others is known as Family 1; the manuscripts in this family share certain common characteristics, such as the omission of Luke 12:40, and the positioning of the story of the adulteress after John 21:25. There is another family headed by cursive 13 and known as Family 13. The manuscripts in that family have the story of the adulteress after Luke 21:38. Other family groupings have been identified, but they are all on a small scale. Computers may assist attempts to isolate further groupings, but the creation of an overall stemma of manuscripts that incorporates a large family tree with most manuscripts in it is impossible. What this means is that we cannot work back through the family to the earliest ancestors, and from these to the original. The genealogical method of finding the original text of the NT is a non-starter. The archetypes of the family groups that have been isolated do not as a rule prove to be members of larger families and the majority of NT manuscripts do not seem to be members of families at all.

For the bulk of the manuscript tradition, all one can do is to speak of groups not families. Groups of manuscripts are those distinguished by their type of text. Thus Aleph 01 and B 03 together with several other manuscripts have a type of text which seems to be associated with Egypt (specifically Alexandria). It is impossible to exhibit 01 and 03 significantly within a family tree, since the differences are too many and too complex, but this looser federation has been established and generally recognized. Other types of texts have been discerned. D 05 and the Old Latin share common characteristics and are said to belong to a so-called Western type of text. The bulk of later manuscripts are said to belong to the Byzantine text-type, which looks like the result of an official church establishment of a text. A Caesarean text-type has been proposed by some scholars. Other groupings and sub-groupings have been identified. Not all such text-types are universally recognized today, but in broad terms the Alexandrian (or Egyptian), the Western, and the Byzantine groupings are in common currency. Such text-types are only broad groupings but they can be convenient handles. The two texts of Acts, to which we have referred, are conveniently labelled as the Western text of Acts (the longer text) and the Alexandrian text (the usual form of Acts commonly printed). Many textual critics have used these labels in stating their judgement of variant readings. Thus, one will find in the literature a general disapproval of the Byzantine type, a general suspicion of the distinctiveness of the Western type and a general approval of readings that belong to the Alexandrian text-type. In fact, since Westcott and Hort's approval of the Alexandrian type, which they called the 'Neutral Text' (by which they meant it was uncorrupted and close to the original), that value-judgement has attached itself to certain witnesses. However, we should not necessarily be mesmerized by such opinions when we turn to the judging of variants such as those set out in Chapter 4.

3

Editing the New Testament Text

As we have already noted, textual criticism is required because none of the original manuscripts is extant today, and the copies that have survived differ from one another. First, let us restate the problem. Our printed editions of the Greek NT depend on manuscripts. Nowadays all copies of the same printing of a text are identical, but no two manuscripts are identical in text let alone in other matters such as format, contents, decoration etc. Our problem is to arrive at the original text amidst such variety. 'Such variety' we say, not merely because the manuscripts differ in text but also because there are so many variants. From the many variant readings found in our manuscripts we have to try at each point of variation to select the original. In the course of the last 1,900 years an original uniformity has been lost in the copious variety which came into being during centuries of copying. We have to reverse the process. Starting from the infinite variety found in the manuscripts we have to work back to the original uniformity.

Let us assume we have completed the first part of our undertaking and have an adequate assembly of variant readings. What are we to do when we are confronted by the bewildering mass of variants in an apparatus? At each point of variation we have to elicit from this mass the reading we may regard as original. This seems perhaps to involve us in two contrary processes. First, we assemble as many variant readings as we can and then try to reduce them to one again. What do we gain by this curious procedure? We cannot tell when we set out whether the reading we start out with is correct until we have collected its rivals, but we have a reasonable confidence that among the readings which we have collected one of them is the right one. What we have to do is to select this right reading from the variety before us. We have now to consider how we set about this next step.

If you buy a copy of the Greek NT, such as the United Bible

Societies' edition (listed in our Bibliography at the end of this book), the text of that NT does not reproduce the text of any one Greek manuscript (see Plate 11). The printed edition is a mixture of readings selected from a large number of manuscripts. It is, in other words, an eclectic text, created by the editors using certain principles and procedures, choosing one variant from here, another reading from there, and so on. The resultant text is something that never existed as such in any one manuscript. The same can be said of all the edited texts, of which there have been many since printing began. Even the first printed Greek testament – Erasmus' of 1516 – was an eclectic text based on the half dozen manuscripts Erasmus had access to in Basle. Such eclecticism of course extends to our modern translations. It is instructive to read the introductions to our English Bibles to see what it was that the translators were working from. Usually, editors select one particular printed edition of the Greek NT on which to base their translation, although in many cases it seems as if they freely dip into the critical apparatus from time to time to translate the variant rather than the main text. Thus an already eclectic text becomes even more eclectic in translation. For example, the revisers of the NEB began their new edition using the printed Greek text edited by R. V. G. Tasker which had been specially prepared for the original NEB, but in the course of their translations they found themselves using Nestle-Aland's 26th edition of the Greek NT. Another example is the NRSV, which is based on UBS[3], but its editors felt free to deviate from that base text occasionally.

We have seen from the previous chapter that the initial task of a textual critic is to assemble the differences between manuscripts. The next task is to produce from this mass of information a text that approximates to the original words written by the original authors. But just how does one begin? What criteria ought to be followed, what principles adopted? How can any one editor or editorial committee cope with the sheer variety and the overwhelming numbers of manuscripts?

Westcott and Hort in 1881 proposed as a dictum, 'Knowledge of documents should precede final judgement on readings.' What they meant by this statement gives us a hint about the first step in our undertaking. 'Knowledge of documents' may be held to include knowledge of the readings of documents and it is this, with which we have first to provide ourselves. We must know what variant readings our manuscripts contain before we can decide between the readings. Until we have catalogued our manuscripts and assembled the variants from at least the most important of them in a critical apparatus, we cannot begin to sift out the original text with any finality.

What principles are to be applied?

Inevitably in any sphere of scholarly activity differing criteria have been proposed and applied. Some advise that one should go for the readings supported by the majority of manuscripts. If manuscripts are divided ought we to accept the reading with the largest support? Should we merely count heads? There is indeed a Greek testament that does claim to represent the text of the majority of manuscripts. This is *The Greek New Testament According to the Majority Text* (see Plate 12). Such an approach is sometimes defended in certain quarters with the claim that divine providence protected Holy Writ by preserving it in large numbers of manuscripts. Until 1881 the usual printed Greek New Testaments on the market were based on the Byzantine text of the medieval church. The earliest printed Greek New Testaments give a text approximating to the readings of the majority of manuscripts. One edition in 1633 claims in its preface to contain 'the text which is now *received by all* in which we give nothing changed or corrupted'. From that meaningless advertising comes the phrase 'Textus Receptus', which in common usage is applied to all early printed Greek New Testaments. In various guises this *Textus Receptus* (TR) dominated the scholarly world for over 350 years. One can understand why it was that after it was eventually toppled from its pedestal when Westcott and Hort's edition was published in 1881 – a text at odds with the TR in many respects – there was a tremendous outcry. That outcry is reflected in the English-speaking world with the furore that greeted the arrival of the Revised Version (RV) of the King James Bible (AV). Many people dedicated themselves to preserving the primacy of the familiar AV in public worship and private reading. In fact, many of the differences in the NT text (as opposed to merely the modernizing of the English usage and style) between the AV and the RV may in broad terms be said to be the differences between the TR and Westcott and Hort's edition. The TR has a fuller text, longer and more complete, when compared with the 1881 Greek text from which the RV was translated. (That 1881 text used by the revisers was very close to Westcott and Hort's.) It was the loss from the NT of certain well-loved verses that caused the greatest outcry from English readers. Some of these variations between a longer and a shorter text are noted in Chapter 4.

There are two problems that make us hesitate to accept what seems to be the democratic solution. One is that the bulk of manuscripts comes from a fairly narrow spectrum of the church. The medieval manuscripts, for the most part, represent the relatively standardized, ecclesiastically approved, version used in the Orthodox Church. Moreover, the Greek-speaking world had shrunk since the earliest Christian centuries, when Greek was the common language in most of the Mediterranean areas into which Christianity spread. Second, we must remember the comment made in Chapter 1 that ultimately in every instance of textual variation the choice is between one reading taken as original and the other reading or readings deemed secondary. In any one instance the copies descended from that original text may be few in number, whereas, because of the hazards of survival, copies descended from the corrupt, secondary, texts, may be very numerous. So, in every variation unit our choice should be not between a reading that may be supported by, let us say, 200 witnesses and one supported by, say, only a dozen, but between two or more separate and different readings, only one of which goes back to the original.

If following the readings of the majority is not wise as a principle, why not instead accept the readings found in our oldest manuscripts? On the face of it that seems sensible. It could be argued that there would be less opportunity for contaminating a text found in third- or fourth-century manuscripts than one found in manuscripts of a much later date. But, again, the logic of that argument is flawed. It may be true that each recopying of a manuscript introduces new and more errors but we do not know how many stages separate any of our extant manuscripts from the original, that is the autograph. It is possible that a tenth-century manuscript is the only surviving copy of, say, a sixth-century manuscript that itself is only two or three stages removed from the original, whereas a fourth-century manuscript could be ten copying generations removed from the original. In any case, it is likely that most deliberate changes would have been introduced into the manuscripts in the first couple of centuries, that is before the NT had acquired the status of canonical scripture, and prior to the time in which most of our surviving manuscripts were written. In other words, the NT was already corrupted even before the date of most of our earliest surviving witnesses. Once the NT was treated as canonical, scribes – or more precisely the churches for which they were producing the text – would have been less tempted to tamper with it. (Careless errors would, of course, continue, as in all copying.) In fact, most of the genuine variants we have – as opposed to orthographical or palaeographical slips – are found in our earliest witnesses. It is not the case that one finds an increasing number of new variants in manuscripts of later centuries.

There are some people who still prefer to go for readings found in the majority of manuscripts. Indeed an international Majority Text Society based in the USA exists to promote this cause. There are others who favour the readings of the great fourth-century codexes (Codex Sinaiticus and Codex Vaticanus) or the early papyri. However, text-critical decisions based exclusively on any of these criteria are flawed. So where do we go from here?

The majority of practising textual critics and editors of scholarly editions in the past thirty years or so now claim to be 'eclectic' critics, by which is meant that they prefer a reading that has a good range of manuscript support (however 'good' is to be defined) and a reading compatible with its context but which seems to have been the cause for the secondary readings being developed. 'Good' usually means a combination of early, Alexandrian-type manuscripts, some papyri, and a wide geographical spread of witnesses including versional and patristic sources. If such a combination supports a reading that on grounds of intrinsic probability is likely to have come from the original author, then that is a reading most editors would print for the original text. If that sort of support exists – and of course in many cases the documentary support is not always so strong or unambiguous – then the textual critic who is of the school of reasoned eclecticism can print the reading with confidence. If you consult the UBS Greek NT it will be seen that each variation unit printed is prefaced with a letter of the alphabet running from 'A' to 'D'. (See Plate 11.) 'A' means that the reading accepted as the original and therefore printed in the text is included with a high degree of confidence, usually because the reading deemed to be original on internal grounds is also well supported by the right mixture of manuscripts. 'B' and 'C' indicate decreasing degrees of certainty and a 'D' reading is printed in the text with little confidence, sometimes because the favoured manuscripts are divided in their attestation or because the nature of the alternative readings is such that a convincing solution is difficult to reach.

Let us return to the term 'intrinsic probability' referred to in the last paragraph. The term usually refers to the internal considerations applied when searching for a reading that fits the language, style, theological stance or context of the book. A reading contrary to the language of the author's usage elsewhere or a theological idea that seems to represent the thinking of a period later than the first century would be unlikely to be original. Other considerations to be looked at are palaeographical and transcriptional, that is the appearance of the written text; is there anything which would encourage accidental change? For example, a combination of similar looking letters in close proximity could facilitate accidental shortening. And what about the nature of the variants presented? For instance, is there one particular reading that could be the progenitor of the others because its Christology (to take an obvious area) cries out for alteration or interpretation? All these considerations are relevant. It is clear that some correctors were very interested in grammar, theology and clarity of expression and they endeavoured to improve the text with these ends in view. Readers also had preferences for particular words which they tended to introduce, whereas they disliked other words which they tended either to replace by synonyms or delete. This is an extension of what many scholars would find evident in the way Matthew and Luke used Mark.

When the text of the Synoptic Gospels (Matthew, Mark and Luke) was being copied, the church encouraged scribes to assimilate the many parallels to be found in these Gospels, usually by harmonizing the words of Mark or Luke to the wording in Matthew with which they were familiar. Similarly, scribes were encouraged to harmonize OT quotations in the NT to the wording in the Greek OT (the Septuagint). In addition, a church may have had particular theological or doctrinal interests and endeavoured to doctor the text with these in mind. Around 200 AD Tertullian, the African church Father, blamed the heretic Marcion for doing this, but we are not to suppose that Marcion was the only one.

In the sentences above we use the words 'tended' and 'endeavoured' because what is quite clear throughout the whole gamut of textual variants in the NT is that prejudices and preferences did not succeed in imposing in a thoroughgoing way a uniform set of corrections. Not all correctors were similarly motivated. Many changes were erratic and piecemeal. The art of copying is essentially highly conservative. The aim is not a formal editorial rewriting. If changes were introduced deliberately they were not introduced exhaustively in all instances by all witnesses. And that is another reason for our being optimistic that the original text has survived somewhere in the manuscript tradition. But it does enable us to accept certain readings as original and certain other types as secondary. For instance, when there are parallel passages in the Synoptic Gospels we would prefer a reading that keeps the parallels dissimilar over against a harmonizing variant that makes parallels agree. The same applies to variants which adapt OT quotations in the NT to the Septuagint: variants that are not harmonized are likely to be what the original author wrote. In the next chapter some variants that seem to have arisen out of assimilation to a parallel are included in a separate section.

Another principle based on internal considerations is less commonly accepted; this says that scribes tended to shorten accidentally the text they were copying rather like heavily laden travellers, who lose a piece of luggage each time they change trains. Although there are clear places where a text has been lengthened by the addition of explanatory words and glosses, in general, omission is a common slip among scribes. Addition requires conscious effort. In the past the maxim 'The shorter text is to be preferred' was regularly cited, and there are some textual critics who still prefer that principle, but the opposite 'The *longer* text is to be preferred' seems a better principle provided the contents, language and style of that longer text are compatible with the rest of the author's writings. In the examples in the following chapter the bulk of the variants do indeed concern a choice between a longer and a shorter text. Most of the textual footnotes in our English versions concern addition and omission. Sometimes we will argue for the originality of the shorter text, but, in general, the longer readings seem to us to be more likely to represent what our biblical authors wrote.

Yet another popular principle is that the harder reading is to be preferred, other things being equal. This principle assumes that, if a reader was confronted with a knotty problem, he would try to improve the text and clarify the meaning. This too is a principle that needs to be borne in mind when assessing textual variation, although, like all these principles, it ought not to be applied mechanically. The rider 'other things being equal' is intended to disqualify readings which are out of character with our author, and readings whose difficulty is so great as to be impossible – one assumes that the original authors always wrote sense, however obscure some sentences may be.

It is the combination of convincing arguments based on internal probability and reliable external evidence (i.e. manuscripts and quotations) that most textual critics look for. Sometimes both are found, but where there is a conflict of interests, perhaps when the arguments based on internal considerations lead to a reading deemed to be weakly supported, then difficult editorial decisions have to be taken. The editors of the UBS text, as we have seen, display their dilemmas in the 'C' and 'D' rankings they print in the apparatus. This text and the Nestle-Aland Greek testament reveal, in their use of square brackets around words, other places where the committee was unable to reach a satisfactory, clear-cut decision. The many bracketed words in these texts mean that there are competing reasons favouring the exclusion or the addition of those words. Such dilemmas are not peculiar to those supporting this eclectic method of approaching textual problems. Those favouring the cult of the best manuscripts, like Westcott and Hort, inevitably reach an impasse if their favourite manuscripts divide, one supporting one reading, the other an alternative. Even the Majority Text, so called because it is a text based on the bulk of manuscripts (in practice the vast number of medieval, Byzantine cursives with a few uncials), is sometimes divided within itself. It does not give a united text throughout. So, in those places, even the editors of the recent printed edition of the Majority Text (listed in our Bibliography) had to make decisions about which part of the evidence to accept as the original.

The radical eclecticism advocated in numerous articles and books on textual criticism by the late G. D. Kilpatrick and by the co-author of the present book, J. K. Elliott, argues that the reading which fits the first-century language and the style of the author, and the reading which best explains the origin of the secondary texts, ought to be printed regardless of the alleged weight of manuscript support. In theory, this approach to textual decision-making is prepared to print a reading supported by only a few, possibly late, cursives if that reading can be justified on internal grounds. Many reviewers of this method are unhappy to accept such a radical line even where they appreciate and accept the internal criteria applied. In the present book this approach will not be emphasized – despite personal temptation to do otherwise. In the practical examples set out in the next chapter we shall try to be as neutral as possible in assessing the variants and no one set of text-critical principles will be consistently advocated or applied.

Whatever one's assessment of the manuscript evidence, all critics need to explain how and why the variants arose. To do so, the principles of intrinsic probability based on internal considerations need to be recognized. As will be readily appreciated from the qualifiers attached to the principles discussed above, rules of textual criticism make for an inexact science. However, text-critical decisions need not be subjective. They are based on principles, but there is room for debate about the relative weight and appropriateness of these principles.

We turn in Chapter 4 to discuss a representative selection of variants. There a brief commentary on each variation unit is intended merely to show the kinds of arguments and principles that can be applied to the variant in question. The suggested solutions ought not to be taken as final or definitive. Some are only starting points for what needs to be a full investigation. Many text-critical problems merit, and some receive, very full discussions in learned articles in scholarly journals. Some are referred to in detailed notes in critical commentaries. Most need to be discussed fully using the Greek text. But our present context allows us only to spotlight a handful of variants taken from the footnotes of current English versions. Many more could have been selected, but we trust that this small sample will encourage readers of the English NT to consider the nature and importance of those alternative readings in the margin prefaced by words such as 'Other manuscripts have . . .'

4

Textual Problems

Some indication has already been given in Chapter 3 of the kind of problem which faces textual critics in the twofold task of trying

  a) to decide what was written in the original text of
      the Greek NT writings;
and
  b) to indicate the reasons which gave rise to
      each variant.

Ideally this chapter would contain an entry for every variant which appears in the footnotes of RSV, JB, NEB, REB, NIV and other important modern English versions, but such an extensive treatment is beyond the scope of this volume. We have, therefore, limited the investigation to variant readings chosen from various parts of the NT for which footnotes appear in modern English versions and these can be used as sample illustrations. Occasionally we indicate the English version where the footnote appears. This has not been done in an exhaustive way throughout the examples cited. Generally, NRSV has the fullest set of footnotes and is the best edition to use for text-critical work using an English translation.

It is worth remembering that the situation is more complicated in the Gospels than it is in the rest of the NT. This is due to a variety of reasons, but mainly it is because there are more manuscripts of the Gospels and because in this area many complications arise from cross-fertilization or harmonization among the four Gospels.

There are basically three types of change that may be introduced when copying a text:

1) Addition/omission.
2) Substitution of one word for another.
3) Word order.

To these could be added dialect changes (affecting the spelling) and the introduction of glosses brought into the text from the margin.

Examples of these are discussed in the sections below. Variants are grouped under the following headings according to characteristics they have in common.

A) Longer or shorter text under the heading 'Addition/ Omission'.

B) Substitution.

C) Changes that concern theology or Christology.

D) Changes involving proper names.

E) Changes of all sorts where harmonization may have been at work (under the heading 'Assimilation').

F) Changes concerning the Greek.

G) A brief indication of some variants that require specialist attention.

H) Word Order.

I) Punctuation.

The discussions are often brief. Sometimes we can do no more than hint at a solution to the problem, either because scholarly consensus has not been reached or because to describe the matter in a definitive way would merit a discussion requiring a learned paper. Sometimes, a full investigation can only be realistically and properly conducted on the basis of the Greek, especially where detailed linguistic or statistical arguments concerning the author's style or linguistic usage come into play.

A) *Addition/Omission*

As one works through a critical apparatus, it is obvious that the largest number of variants concern a choice between a longer or a shorter text, a word added here, a word omitted there. It is easy to collect a couple of hundred such variants even in the very selective number of footnotes in an English edition. Obviously variants of this kind affect translation. An old maxim applied to textual decisions was that the shorter reading is to be preferred, but a stronger case can be made for preferring the originality of a longer text. If one is copying a long document by hand it is obviously very easy to omit words accidentally. The kinds of mistakes modern copy-typists make reveal how omission is a common error. Such errors can often be explained if there is a visual reason why an accidental shortening of the text in the exemplar was facilitated.

In theologically sensitive texts we shall also come across cases where it seems as if the original has been deliberately shortened in order to avoid a word or phrase about which some early readers may have felt repugnance.

Harmonization of two parallel passages, one of which is shorter than the other, may have resulted in either the shorter parallel being added to in order to make the passage agree with the longer, or the longer being shortened to make it conform with the shorter. Sometimes the two parallels could both have variants harmonizing their readings in differing directions. At each point one needs to weigh up which is the likelier direction of change.

Some additions may be liturgical. Ecclesiastical influence may have caused certain readings to be introduced – theological titles, doxologies and the like. On very rare occasions explanatory glosses (some originally intended only for the margins of the manuscript) also crept into the text.

Let us turn first i) to two examples where textual variants concern the addition or omission of whole passages, then ii) to whole verses and, finally, iii) to smaller cases of addition/omission.

i) The only two major sections in the NT that are disputed are the ending of Mark's Gospel and the story of the adulteress.

First Mark. Older English translations take the Gospel up to 16:20. In the nineteenth century, after Vaticanus had been published in a critical edition and Sinaiticus had been discovered, the scholarly world had two new manuscripts much respected by Westcott and Hort and highly influential as witnesses to the biblical text: these two manuscripts, virtually alone among Greek witnesses, lack Mark 16:9–20. NIV refers to these as 'the most reliable early manuscripts'. (Some Coptic, Syriac, Armenian and Georgian manuscripts support these two Greek uncials in the omission of this passage, as do some Fathers.) Their witness has meant that nearly all English translations since 1881, with the exception of those which follow the AV, do not have the last twelve verses of Mark. Usually the verses are printed within brackets, in the margin or in a different typeface. These devices are intended by the translators to signify that they agree with the prevailing text-critical judgement that these verses, although well-known, were never part of the original text of Mark. The result is that Mark's Gospel ends very abruptly with the fear and disobedience of the women, and it ends peculiarly, some would even say uniquely, with the Greek particle *gar* ('for', 'because'). Books and many articles and theses have been devoted to the problem. It seems clear to us that, as it stands, 16:9–20 was not written by the same author as the rest of the Gospel – language, style, and theological content brand it as non-Markan. Any solutions to the problem of what happened to the original ending, assuming Mark would never have intended originally to finish his Gospel at verse 8, must be purely speculative. But it does seem as if at an early date this ending (and also another, shorter, ending) were concocted, largely out of other Easter stories, to provide Mark with a suitable conclusion.

Now to the Adulteress. This famous story has been printed conventionally as part of the Fourth Gospel, where it is usually numbered John 7:53–8:11, although there are at least five other locations where it is sited in various manuscripts, including the end of Luke 21. There is great textual variety within the story itself, there being some six or seven differing accounts in our manuscripts. But there is also a sizable number of other manuscripts, including those that have exercised greatest influence, such as early papyri, Codex Vaticanus and Codex Sinaiticus, that lack the story anywhere. As when assessing the originality of the ending of Mark, internal investigations have been appealed to when analysing the story of the adulteress and these reveal that the language and style of the story are alien to John, and indeed to Luke. The story, famous and beloved though it is, is nonetheless no part of the original NT. It is a piece of early floating Christian tradition, comparable to some of the sayings and stories of the apocryphal Gospels. As such, it has no place in our printed NT, although modern editions usually include it, bracketed, in a margin, or as an appendix.

ii) There are other lengthy passages which are in some manuscripts but not in others. It surprises people just how many complete verses, especially in the Gospels, are absent from some manuscripts. Let us first of all list them: Matthew 6:13b; 9:34; 12:47; 16:2–3; 17:21; 18:11; 21:44; 23:14; 27:35b, 49b; Mark 7:16; 9:44, 46; 11:26; 15:28; Luke 5:39; 11:4b; 17:36; 22:19b–20, 43–44; 23:17, 34a; 24:6, 9 [from the tomb], 12, 36 [and he said to them, Peace to you], 40, 51 [and was taken into heaven], 52 [worshipping (him)]; John 5:3b–4; Acts 8:37; 10:30; 15:34; 24:6b–8a; 28:16, 29; Romans 14:23–7; 16:20b, (24); 1 Corinthians 15:54; 1 John 5:7–8. (The words in square brackets are disputed in the textual transmission of the verse.)

Space does not permit a full discussion of all of these, often famous, passages. The footnotes to most English editions include these variants. The questions the critic needs to ask are: Are the words in the longer passage compatible with the language, usage and theology of the author? Could the omission have been facilitated by palaeographical considerations, homoeoteleuton and the like? Could the disputed words have been added/omitted through assimilation to a parallel? Applying these and comparable criteria, as well as keeping an eye on the significance of the manuscript support for the variants, one could conclude, for example, that Matthew 9:34 was added by harmonization to Matthew 12:24 or Luke 11:15. Other verses, possibly added from a parallel passage, are Matthew 17:21 (from Mark 9:29); Matthew 18:11 (from Luke 19:10); Matthew 27:49b (from John 19:34, although a case can be made for the originality of the verse in Matthew, especially in view of its position in the story of Jesus' death – as it stands, this longer text in Matthew differs from John's account by having Jesus pierced prior to his death).

Homoeoteleuton may have accidentally created the shorter text at Matthew 12:47; 21:44; 23:14; 27:35b; Mark 11:26; 15:28; Luke 17:36; 1 Corinthians 15:54. (Matthew 23:14 in some manuscripts appears after verse 12; again, omission through homoeoteleuton would still apply, but, as we have already seen – and we will see further examples shortly – when a disputed reading appears in differing positions its originality *anywhere* in the book is open to question.) Harmonization could also account for the omission of Mark 15:28; the comparable sentence is not found in the parallel passage in Luke (although a similar sentence appears elsewhere in Luke).

Occasionally a longer text looks as if it contains an explanatory gloss. Matthew 16:2–3 has that appearance, although to reject the originality of these verses is to do so on the evidence principally of Vaticanus and Sinaiticus. John 5:3b–4 is a stronger candidate as an addition to the Gospel.

One might have thought that the Lord's Prayer, of all passages, was a text that would have been transmitted accurately as it was familiar to the scribes. But not at all! The textual tradition is very confused, suggesting not only that the prayer was differently remembered in various Christian circles, but that it was not recorded as an immutable piece of teaching. Not only are the two versions, Matthew's and Luke's, different from one another – for example Matthew's is commonly printed with seven petitions, Luke's with only five – but the forms in which both accounts were copied vary in the manuscript tradition. Obviously, some variants are due to attempts to assimilate one Gospel's account to the other, but variants within Luke alone create at least four fundamentally different versions of the prayer. Some variants are mere pious expansions due to liturgical influence, but there are two substantial variants where we are dealing with a longer or shorter text. One is the end of the prayer in Matthew. Does Matthew 6:13 end with the subscription '. . . for thine is the kingdom . . .' or not? The other is at Luke 11:4 where some manuscripts add 'but deliver us from evil'. The former is likely to have been due to liturgical influence, the latter to assimilation to the Matthaean form.

Luke 22:19b–20, containing Jesus' closing words over the eucharistic bread and his saying over the cup, is a passage about which defenders of the shorter and defenders of the longer text have spilt much ink. The question whether or not Luke included these words during his account of the Last Supper is too important to be discussed in a cursory manner. To do the textual problem justice one would need to examine other accounts of the institution of the Eucharist in the NT and in early Christianity. Also one would need to examine the longer text from the point of view of Lukan language and theology – including a full examination of the textual complexities in verses 17 to 20 as a whole. A decisive argument on one side might be the unlikelihood of these sacred words being deliberately excised if they stood in the text originally, and the probability of their being added later to make Luke have a saying over the cup to follow the saying over the bread.

Jesus' forgiveness of (presumably) the Romans 'for they know not what they do' in Luke 23:34 is also a much disputed case. Were the words added from a gloss, or removed either after the Romans fell into disfavour with Christians, or because the words were interpreted as forgiving the *Jews*?

The variants in the final chapter of Luke (24:3, 6, 12, 36, 40, 51, 52), some involving a full verse, are often considered together. As this strange string of omissions is attested by Western manuscripts, principally Codex Bezae, that is by witnesses which are usually perceived to be expanders of the NT text, the tendency among scholars has been to accept the Western readings here but to reject the longer readings in these manuscripts elsewhere (such as the longer Western glosses at John 5:3b–4; Acts 8:37, where there are at least eight forms of the variant in manuscripts including the verse: 10:30; 15:34; 24:6b–8a; 28:16, 29 to take some striking longer additions, all of which are in AV). The peculiar phrase 'Western non-interpolations' was given rather arbitrarily to these seven variants in Luke 24 (and two elsewhere – Matthew 27:49b; Luke 22:19b–20) by Westcott and Hort, although the opposite, 'non-Western interpolations', might have been better. In any case, nowadays, scholars are not always as prepared as they once were to accept that these disputed additions are all secondary to Luke. For example, Luke 24:51. This is an important text. The relation between the end of Luke and the beginning of Acts is a matter for debate. Has the Gospel as well as Acts an account of the Ascension? The key clause in the Gospel is 24:51 'and he was taken up into heaven', but this is absent from some manuscripts. How are we to account for the variation? The omission could have been accidental, facilitated by the Greek word for 'and' which prefaces this clause and the verse following. Various editors and translators are receptive to the originality of this and the other non-Western interpolations. The old consensus in favour of D (Codex Bezae) here has broken down. Each addition now needs to be looked at on its own merits. In some instances it may nevertheless still be concluded that D is right after all. For example, Luke 24:12, in which Peter looks into the tomb, could be an addition to Luke from John's Easter story. On the other hand the story in John could have developed from Luke 24:12. If the verse were original to Luke one would then have to explain how the omission in D came about.

In Luke 22:43–44 the angelic support for Jesus and the reference to his bloody sweat may have been omitted through assimilation to the parallels which lack this detail in their accounts of the agony in Gethsemane – if so, that would be an instance where assimilation results in a shortening of the text – but it is more likely that these verses, original to Luke, were omitted because some early Christians rejected their contents as giving too 'human' a picture of Jesus and unsuitable in their Christology.

In Mark 7:16 the stylized formula 'He who has ears to hear let him hear' is omitted by some manuscripts, but is likely to be original. This same formula occurs at Matthew 11:15; 13:9, 43 but the verb 'to hear' is not found in all the manuscripts. The variants are shown in NRSV. Was this such a formalized, fixed expression that authors repeated it in exactly the same way each time, or was it the kind of formula that later copyists standardized in their copies?

The phrase '. . . where their worm never dies and the fire is never quenched', read in all manuscripts at Mark 9:48, is repeated in some manuscripts as verses 44 and 46. The repetition gives the passages the nature of a rhythmic and formal incantation that speaks in favour of the originality of the disputed verses as part of Mark's Gospel.

The ending of Romans, like the ending of Mark, betrays textual confusion. Some manuscripts have a doxology, either at Romans 14:23–7, or at the end of chapter 16, or, in one early papyrus only (P^{46}), at the end of chapter 15. Some give it in two locations, at the end of 14 and 16. Whenever one finds variants in differing positions one is often justified in looking upon that reading as secondary. Here the doxology does not belong to Pauline language and style, and seems to be a liturgical addition placed in various positions – possibly reflecting whether the epistle circulated with 14, 15 or 16 chapters. These words are unlikely to have been omitted at some stage if they were original.

A benediction is sometimes added and numbered Romans 16:20b, although in some manuscripts it appears as 16:24 and in others it follows 16:27. Again, the fluctuating positions make one suspicious about its originality. However, all the manuscripts have the benediction somewhere in the chapter. One could perhaps argue that the benediction is an addition found in all manuscripts. The words could have been added to round off the passage when it was read in church. To argue along these lines takes one into the area of conjectural emendation – a topic covered in our Postscript.

We noted above a few Western additions to the text of Acts. The whole problem of the text of Acts is a major problem for textual criticism – perhaps the most important. The point is that Acts comes in two forms, basically Western and non-Western (or Alexandrian) as far as manuscript allegiances are concerned. In the past, these additions and explanatory glosses have been dismissed *en bloc* as secondary and due to a rewriting by the scribe of Codex Bezae. More recently, it has been recognized that many of the variants are found in sources older than D and could not have arisen with a late, say, fourth century, rewriting of Acts. Also, it is recognized that many of these longer additions have characteristically Lukan turns of phrase and language. As a result of this research, it may well be that what we have in the so-called Western text of Acts is a rewriting by *Luke* of Acts, that is to say a revised reissue of the original that we read in our usual printed editions. So, for Acts, uniquely in the NT, the task of textual critics might be not to establish one original text but two different 'original' versions of that same text. It also means that the Western readings cannot be dismissed automatically, but that each must be weighed and treated on its merits. So, the readings we listed above (Acts 8:37; 10:30; 15:34; 24:6b–8a; 28:16, 29) as secondary should be reconsidered, along with large numbers of other additions, as possibly belonging to Luke's revision of his own work. Metzger's *Commentary* has a helpful introduction to this vexed question of the two texts of Acts, as well as discussions of many of the variants. Another helpful guide to Acts (and to other disputed passages in the Greek NT) is C. S. C. Williams, *Alterations to the Text of the Synoptic Gospels and Acts* (Oxford: Blackwell, 1951 especially chapter V). A convenient presentation of the two Greek texts printed on facing pages is to be found in F. J. Foakes Jackson and Kirsopp Lake, *The Beginnings of Christianity* (London: Macmillan, 1926) Vol. 3: J. H. Ropes, *The Text of Acts.* See also J. M. Wilson, *The Acts of the Apostles. Translated from the Codex Bezae* (London: SPCK, 1923).

'There are three that testify [in heaven, the Father, the Word, and the Holy Spirit, and these three are one. And there are three that testify on earth], the Spirit and the water and the blood and these three agree'. The three heavenly witnesses in 1 John 5:7–8 are well known to readers of the AV, but the disputed words, bracketed above, are found, as NIV points out (in a rare example of citing manuscript attestation for its marginal variants) only in late Vulgate manuscripts. The passage, known as the *Comma Johanneum,* seems to have originated in the Latin tradition, from which it was translated into Greek – it is found in a couple of late Greek manuscripts. ('*Comma*' here is a technical term meaning a single phrase or sense line.) Because the words appear in the Clementine edition of the Latin Vulgate, the Roman Catholic Church has, until recently, been reluctant to deny the authenticity of the words as part of this epistle.

iii) We now turn to smaller, but no less important, variants involving addition or omission. Space does not permit a full discussion of each but the following are worthy of attention, and are symptomatic of the kind of changes copyists created. We merely offer suggested solutions, but the passages merit fuller consideration before a final decision can be pronounced. Consultation of the questionable passages ought to be undertaken with scholarly commentaries. Those omissions likely to have been prompted by homoeoteleuton, that is, the accidental shortening of a text facilitated by the similar spelling of two neighbouring words, are dealt with first. (In many other instances an addition or an omission has been caused through assimilation to a parallel version of the same sentence elsewhere in the NT – such variants are grouped together below under E.)

OMISSIONS PROMPTED BY HOMOEOTELEUTON

If an omission is likely to have been caused by the accidental shortening of the text through homoeoteleuton we will be disposed to accept the originality of the longer text, provided of course that the longer text is compatible with the author's writing elsewhere, and that there are no stronger competing arguments favouring the short text and capable of explaining how the lengthening of the text arose. (In most instances one can see the palaeographical reasons for the shortening of the text only if one examines the Greek.) The following is a sample of verses where the longer text, bracketed in the quotation, is likely to be original, but was accidentally omitted through homoeoteleuton by some scribes (or, more probably *once* by *one* scribe, from whose carelessly produced copy all subsequent shortened copies descended):

Mark 10:7: 'And for this reason a man shall leave his father and his mother and [unite with his wife and] the two will become one'. The omission makes nonsense of the passage, but it can be explained as an accident, facilitated by homoeoteleuton, because the text omitted is preceded in Greek by the words 'his and' and itself ends with those two words. It would have been easy for a careless scribe to jump from the first 'his and' to the second, thereby omitting the passage bracketed above.

The following passages also contain variants where the shorter text could have come about through homoeoteleuton:

Matthew 12:15:	'. . . Many [crowds] followed him . . .' (NAV, NRSV)
Matthew 14:30:	'. . . [strong] wind . . .' (NAV, NRSV)
Mark 1:40:	'A leper came to him, imploring him, [and kneeling before him] . . .' (NRSV)

Mark 3:32:	'. . . and your brothers [and your sisters] . . .' (NRSV)
Luke 17:24:	'. . . for the Son of Man [in his day] . . .' (NIV)
Luke 22:16:	'. . . I shall not [ever] eat . . .' (NRSV, REB)
John 5:44:	'. . . the only (One) [God]' (NIV)
John 13:32:	'[If God is glorified in him,] then God will glorify the Son in himself . . .' (NIV, NRSV, REB)
1 Corinthians 13:1–2:	'. . . I do not have love [I have become a noisy gong or a clanging cymbal. And if I have prophetic powers, and understand all mysteries and all knowledge, and if I have all faith so as to remove mountains but do not have love], I am nothing.' (See Plate 2.)
2 Corinthians 11:3:	'. . . [purity] and single-hearted devotion' (NAV, NRSV, REB)
Revelation 13:7:	'[And it was given to him to make war on the saints and to conquer them.] And it was given to him to have authority . . .' (NRSV)

OTHER INSTANCES OF ADDITION/OMISSION

Mark 8:26: 'Do not even go into the village [or speak to anyone in the village]'. The longer text is often seen as a conflate reading combining two shorter alternatives 'Do not go into the village' and 'Do not speak to anyone in the village'. But the longer text in which Jesus, strangely, tells the man not to enter the village nor speak to any one in the village, could be the 'father' of the two shorter forms. Mark is fond of these redundant expressions and doublets.

Mark 8:38: 'If a person is ashamed of me and mine (i.e. my people/disciples) . . .' or 'If a person is ashamed of me and my words . . .' The Greek involves either the absence or presence of the word 'words'. It is a variant relatively straightforward to explain and resolve, using Mark's proven linguistic style. In Mark, as indeed in Luke too, there is a rule for the possessives 'mine', 'yours', etc. They can be used like the English 'mine' pronominally or predicatively, but, when an attributive possessive is required corresponding to the English 'my', the genitive form of the possessive pronoun, 'of me', is used. This means that Mark could have written 'mine' or 'the words of me' but not 'my words'. That being so, 'mine', meaning 'my disciples', must be right. The same holds true for the parallel passage (Luke 9:26) where a similar variation occurs and where we should also read 'mine'.

Mark 9:49: 'Everyone will be salted with fire [and every sacrifice will be salted with salt].' The general tendency has been to reject the longer text, found in the majority of manuscripts, because of the prejudice against the alleged conflating tendency of the Byzantine text-type, but, if the longer text were original, one could then explain the origin of the two shortened versions – the shorter text, shown here, and another variant that has substituted the bracketed words for the unbracketed.

Mark 12:23: '. . . in the Resurrection, [when they are raised]. . .' This apparently unnecessary clause is typical of Mark's style. It is not good Greek and was therefore readily jettisoned by stylistically conscious scribes. The words, like several other redundant expressions in Mark, are likely to be original to the Gospel.

Luke 9:54–56. Three variants hang together here: (54 at end) '. . . [just as Elijah did]; (55 at end) [And he said, "You do not know (*or* Do you not know) what kind of spirit you are of; (56 at beginning) for the Son of Man did not come to destroy men's lives, but to save them."] Are these additions from an extraneous source or original to Luke's account? Verses 52 to 56 are peculiar to Luke so assimilation is not an issue. Might it be that the words were omitted because they are derogatory to the disciples? There is much hesitation in the commentaries about the status of these disputed words.

Acts 15:20, 29. In our printed texts the Apostolic Decree warns Christians against four things, idolatry, fornication, that which is strangled, and blood. Several manuscripts omit the reference to things strangled. Thus if 'blood' here means murder, the shorter text is a Decree where the stress is ethical. (Such an interpretation is reinforced by some manuscripts which add at verse 20 and at verse 29 the negative form of the Golden Rule found in Matthew 7:12.) Some other manuscripts omit the reference to fornication but include the reference to things strangled; there the Decree can be interpreted as emphasizing ceremonial requirements if 'blood' means the avoidance of eating meat with blood in it. The text with the four prohibitions combines ethical and ceremonial law. We may suppose that the two shorter forms represent separate attempts to introduce greater consistency into the Decree, one by eliminating the most distinctive ethical element and the other by eliminating the most ceremonial. Naturally the whole question whether the Decree was food law or moral law – or a mixture – has given rise to an extensive body of literature. That the same variants occur on the two occasions where the Decree is set out shows that the alterations were deliberate.

Romans 8:28. If the addition of 'God' is read with Papyrus 46, Alexandrinus and Vaticanus, then it is the subject of the verb 'works', and the meaning is: 'God works all things together for good'. If the shorter text is read with Sinaiticus, Claromontanus and the majority of manuscripts, then the word 'all' becomes the subject and the meaning is: 'All things work together for good', a more difficult concept – (is Paul the universal optimist?) – and one that may have encouraged the change in text, even though 'God' earlier in the verse then becomes redundant.

Ephesians 1:1: 'From Paul . . . to God's people [in Ephesus].' If this was originally a general letter then the address may be a later addition; if the letter was originally sent to Ephesus the specific address would be removed when it became a circular later (cf. Romans 1:7 [in Rome], 15 [to those in Rome]). Sinaiticus (first hand, that is, the writing of the original scribe of the manuscript and not that of a later corrector), Vaticanus (first hand) and Papyrus 46 omit the words, and, because these are manuscripts highly regarded by most textual critics, their testimony has been carefully considered. Note that the correctors of Sinaiticus and Vaticanus add, or restore, the words. On balance, the direction of change seems to have been away from the specific to the general.

iv) To conclude this section we list a few further interesting cases. To present the evidence objectively we bracket the disputed word or words. One must decide if the words were deliberately excised or added. Did a scribe feel that an additional explanation was required or that the words in the original were superfluous?

Matthew 5:22: '. . . if any one is angry [without cause] . . .'
Mark 3:14: '. . . [whom he named apostles] . . .' Cf. Mark 3:16 '[So he appointed the twelve] . . .'
Luke 11:33: 'No one lights a lamp and then hides it [or puts it under a bowl] . . .'
John 3:31–32: '. . . He who comes from heaven [is above all and] bears witness to what he has seen . . .'

John 4:9:	'. . . [Jews do not share drinking vessels with Samaritans].'
John 13:10:	'Every one who has a bath is completely clean and does not have to wash himself [except for his feet].'
Romans 11:6b:	'[But if it is of works, it is no longer grace; otherwise work is no more work].'
Galatians 2:5:	'Because of false brethren . . . I [never] yielded to them [even] for a short time . . .'
1 Peter 5:2:	'. . . to tend the flock of God that is in your charge [exercising (episcopal) oversight] . . .

B) *Substitution*

Under this heading are included variants where one word or phrase has been replaced by another. As so often, harmonization may be the explanation for some of the changes, but other reasons exist. For example, a particular word may not have struck the copyist as precise enough, or the word may have gone out of fashion (the original, first-century word may not have been in current use when, say, an eighth-century scribe was at work), or a grammatical change seemed to be required. We must not assume that changes were necessarily improvements, but there was a tendency to polish the language and style of the NT, which was not always the best literary Greek. Most of the NT authors were writing Greek as a second language and some of them (Mark, John, the author of the book of Revelation, and the author of the Pastorals) wrote in a rough style with limited vocabulary that invited copyists to make corrections. Some readers in the church were clearly among the learned of their day, schooled in the literary classics; doubtless they baulked at some of the vocabulary and turns of phrase in the NT and therefore had these words changed. To be able to reach convincing decisions on these matters we really need to refer to dictionaries, concordances, grammars and other tools, but in the samples below we can hint where the origin of a variant lies. To resolve many of these types of variant one often needs to take into account the whole context and even the developments of Christian theology or church history before a convincing explanation of the likeliest direction of change can be given.

Mark 1:2. Some manuscripts tell us that the citation is from Isaiah, other manuscripts state that the quotation is written 'in the prophets'. This substitution seems a clear example of a change to correct what was seen as a factual error, because the quotation following is not only from Isaiah but in part from Malachi as well. A pedantic scribe replaced the original 'in Isaiah the prophet' by the accurate 'in the prophets'.

Mark 1:41. Is Jesus 'angry' when approached by the leper, or 'moved with compassion'? Despite the relatively weak attestation for 'angry' this reading is the more difficult reading (although capable of convincing interpretation by exegetes) and the one that would have been avoided. 'Moved with compassion' is a secondary reading.

Mark 7:3. REB has the Pharisees 'washing their hands' and adds as footnotes the alternative readings, adding either 'with the fist' or 'regularly'. Although the latter makes clear sense, it is likely to be secondary to the word that is translated here as 'with the fist'. In fact it is not clear how that word should be translated and what it is that the author is telling us about the washing habits of Pharisees. For that reason the word is likely to be original, but, because of its difficulty, it was substituted by the unobjectionable 'frequently' or omitted. The omission is found in only one Greek witness and it is thus surprising that this is the reading preferred by REB.

Luke 1:46. The Magnificat is normally known as a hymn attributed to the Virgin Mary, but some Latin manuscripts substitute the name 'Elizabeth'. This variant is in the footnotes of REB and NRSV. A good case can be made for the originality of 'Elizabeth' here. As Christianity developed there was a tendency to enhance the role of Mary. Elizabeth parallels the infertile Hannah on whose prayer in 1 Samuel 2 the Lukan song is based. In the context in Luke the hymn ends with the words 'and Mary stayed with her'. The pronoun would read better if the preceding subject had been Elizabeth. However, few critics are willing to accept into the Greek testament a reading known only from versional evidence.

Luke 4:44. NIV alerts us to the substitution of 'Galilee' for 'Judea' at the end of the chapter, but which name was original? Did Jesus keep on preaching in the synagogues of Judea or Galilee? Why the substitution? In the parallel passage in Mark 1: 35–39 all texts agree that Jesus was in Galilee (and cf. Matthew 4:32), so that name could have entered manuscripts of Luke through assimilation. 'Judea' is the more difficult reading because the context makes it clear that

Jesus had been in Galilee. Before we automatically accept the more difficult reading as the original, it is worth asking ourselves if a difficult reading is so inexplicable and problematic that it is more likely to have arisen as a careless scribal blunder rather than be part of the original text.

Luke 10:1, 17. How many disciples did Jesus send out? The manuscripts are divided – some have 'seventy', others 'seventy-two'. There is symbolism in both numbers, but 'seventy' is more common in the OT than 'seventy-two'. It is possible, therefore, that an original 'seventy-two' was altered by scribes to the more frequent 'seventy' than vice versa.

Luke 14:5. Did Jesus speak of 'an ass or an ox' falling into a well or 'a son or an ox'? Several English versions note this bizarre substitution. Other manuscripts conflate all three ('ass', 'son' and 'ox'). Another variant exists reading 'sheep' instead of 'son' (through assimilation to Matthew 12:11). The Greek words for 'son' and 'ass' are not dissimilar in appearance so the substitution could perhaps be due to accidental misreading. If 'son' were original it strikes one as strange – but is this an impossible reading?

1 Corinthians 2:1. Did Paul preach 'the mystery of God' or 'the testimony about God'? Paul could and did use both concepts, but which is more appropriate in the context and why was a change made?

At 1 Corinthians 15:51 a substitution which has significant theological implications has Paul saying: 'We shall all be raised but we shall not all be changed'. That is the reading of D 06 (Codex Claromontanus) instead of the usual: 'We shall not all sleep but we shall all be changed'. (The transfer of the negative to the second clause is another variant here, but one which seems to be secondary, written after Paul and his correspondents had died). The reading of D introduces an idea not found elsewhere in the NT about the fate of the wicked dead, which probably invalidates any claim to its being considered as the original text.

1 Thessalonians 3:2. The variants noted in NIV: 'Timothy . . . our brother and God's fellow-worker' and 'Timothy . . . our brother and God's servant' are but two alternatives out of many variants. The original text (read here by the first hand of Claromontanus) seems to be 'fellow-worker' an idea that caused many changes, such as the substitution of the unobjectionable 'servant', the omission or repositioning of the possessive 'God's' and various conflations.

Thus, in contrast to the preceding variant, we accept here the originality of the text preserved in D virtually alone. Here is one of the many problem cases when assessments on internal probability conflict with considerations based on external evidence.

At Hebrews 2:9 it is likely that the author spoke of Jesus' dying 'without God'. This is a reading, admittedly poorly attested in manuscripts although well represented in patristic citations, that is noted in REB as an alternative to 'by God's grace'. In Greek the words 'by the grace' and 'without' are similar in appearance. The change, though, is likely to have been deliberate in order to remove the puzzling statement that Jesus (of all people) was ever 'without God'. But the idea is consistent with OT ideas about death, and is compatible with NT teaching that in death Jesus was inevitably – albeit temporarily – outside God's realm (cf. the cry of dereliction from the cross in Mark 15:34).

James 2:20. Is faith without works 'useless' (as in some manuscripts) or 'dead' (as in other witnesses)? This variant, noted in GNB and NIV, is another where we must weigh alternative possibilities – an author's consistency, James' use of 'dead' twice elsewhere in this chapter in a similar way (verses 17, 26), or a scribe's conformity of this verse to the other two.

1 Peter 2:21; 3:18. A major theological discussion hinges on the alternatives. Did Christ 'suffer' or 'die' according to the argument in these verses? A deliberate change is most likely but it needs to be recognized that in Greek the one could be accidentally read for the other. However, it seems as if there was an aversion on the part of some scribes to 1 Peter's references to Christ 'suffering'. (Yet another variant avoiding 'suffering' occurs at 4:1.)

2 Peter 2:13. In some manuscripts 'love feasts' is substituted for 'deceits'. NIV notes the variant here but not at Jude 12 where the same variant occurs. Given the close relationship of Jude and 2 Peter, the same word could occur in both books. But if the two books are to be made different here, which text has which word and in which direction are we to see the assimilation? These are the only two passages in the NT which refer to a love feast (in Greek: *agape*) and this may make us hesitate before accepting that the concept belongs in the NT at all. One also needs to note that scribes could have substituted one of the words for the other accidentally as both look alike (*apatais/agapais*).

A few other interesting substitutions may be given briefly. At Luke

23:45 was the sun 'darkened' or 'eclipsed' at the time of the crucifixion? At John 7:8 do we read 'I am not going to this festival' or 'I am not yet going to this festival'? The manuscripts divide between *ouk* (not) and *oupo* (not yet). 'Not' (in Sinaiticus and Bezae) makes Jesus contradict himself – see verse 10 – and thus might be the original, although many critics would prefer the alternative reading *oupo* in Papyri 66 and 75, Vaticanus and the Majority Text. (A similar change from *ou* to *oupo* is seen at Philippians 3:13, a variation noted in GNB: '. . . I really do not [yet] think I have already won it'). At Acts 10:19 there is a confused array of variants: either 'men' are looking for Simon Peter, or 'two men' (the reading by Vaticanus alone, agreeing with Acts 10:7) or 'three men' (as in Acts 11:11). At Romans 9:4 the variants 'covenant' or 'covenants' can be explained in favour of the originality of the more difficult plural, which is likely to have caused theological problems about a multiplicity of covenants.

As a sub-section we include those variants which on the face of it might seem slight or insignificant, but which ought to be analysed just as thoroughly as an ostensibly major variant. Some of these apparently insignificant variants are concerned with pronouns and they, of course, can affect and alter the meaning of the whole section. The moral, of course, is that even relatively small alterations cause significant changes, and are often themselves the result of a differing interpretation of the text from that which was originally intended or understood.

Matthew 17:4. During the Transfiguration does Peter speak personally ('I will make three dwellings here') or does he include his fellow disciples ('We will make . . .')? The manuscripts are divided: NRSV draws our attention to the alternatives. The change between the first singular and the first plural involves only three Greek letters and the alteration could have occurred in either direction. The variant needs to be resolved by the context. Peter has just referred to the three being there and goes on to mention the three tents required for Moses, Elijah and Jesus. Is it likely that he intends each disciple to be responsible for one tent apiece? Or is this an interpretative change introduced by a scribe to a text that had Peter speak only for himself? Alternatively, is the narrowing down of an original plural to the singular due to a later age in which Peter was venerated?

Matthew 18:14: 'So it is not the will of your Father in heaven that one of these little ones should be lost'. Thus NRSV with the footnote drawing our attention to the variant 'our' Father. The difference between 'our' and 'your' in Greek involves the changing of only one letter. (The two words were also probably pronounced identically.) Those words are frequently interchanged throughout the NT in the manuscripts. So the issue must be resolved by the context. Manuscript weight and numbers are not trustworthy guides in variants like this – even for those eclectic critics who try to balance external and internal criteria. Matthew uses both 'my' Father and 'our' Father so we cannot decide this on the basis of the author's practice elsewhere. 'My Father' occurs in 18:10 and 18:35. It may be that these verses were responsible for the change from an original 'your' in verse 14 to 'our'. On the other hand we may prefer to argue that in the context Jesus is speaking throughout of his personal relationship with his Father, in which case we would print 'our' – later to be changed to the inclusive 'your'. Other examples of the our/your interchange may be seen in many variants including the following noted in modern translations: 2 Corinthians 1:11 (NIV); 2 Corinthians 8:7 (NIV, GNB, REB); Colossians 1:7 (GNB, REB); Colossians 2:13 (NIV); Colossians 3:4 (NIV); 1 John 1:4 (GNB, NIV).

Mark 2:16. Are the accusers of Jesus 'scribes and Pharisees' or 'scribes of the Pharisees'? NRSV draws our attention to the variant. 'Scribes of the Pharisees' is the more difficult variant in so far as there is no evidence outside this reading that such a group existed. It probably means scribes who were of the Pharisaic party, but, as an unusual phrase, it would have cried out for alteration, and the minor change 'scribes *and* Pharisees' introduces a common and well understood couple of groups.

Mark 6:14. Several English versions note the variant 'he said' instead of 'people were saying'. The change in Greek is between the third person singular and the third person plural of the verb 'to say' and involves only one letter being altered. The change could have occurred in either direction. However, the plural is required in the context. The sentence begins with Herod hearing of Jesus' fame, but the verb 'to say' refers to the differing opinions about Jesus that Herod had heard. Thus 'they say' is appropriate in the parenthesis. If this was a deliberate change, scribes may have intended, erroneously, to link the verb 'to say' with the earlier singular verb 'he heard'. See also Mark 11:19: 'When evening came they [*or* 'he'] went out of the city'. Only a slight change exists in Greek between the two persons of the verb in this instance. One should consider that the singular is original, and that it was altered to the plural to make a neater bridge with the (originally separate) story beginning in the verse following, where the subject is plural.

Mark 11:24: 'Whatever you ask for in prayer believe you have received it and it will be yours' or '. . . you are receiving . . .'. This variant is noted in NRSV. There is even a third variant involving yet another tense: Codex Bezae and its allies have the future '. . . you will receive . . .'. Which is Mark likely to have written, and how did the alternatives arise? The future probably came about through assimilation to the Matthaean parallel, but what of the others? 'You have received' is the more difficult reading and is the one that scribes are likely to have altered. What looks like a past tense was probably intended by Mark to represent a Semitic tense which implies future action, but later scribes may not have understood this. On the other hand it is worth noting that the present is Mark's favourite tense, and one that he uses excessively.

Another variant involving changes in tense is at Luke 1:78. In the Benedictus does Zechariah prophesy that the dawn from on high 'has broken' upon us or 'will break' upon us? The alternatives are given in NRSV. The hymn begins with the past tense of this same verb. Is the author consistent in using this tense to close it too, or is the change from an original future due to a scribe creating this consistency? This is a common question in textual matters, especially when the variant involves an agreement with the author's practice elsewhere. Is consistency something to be expected of an author, or is it something imposed on an author by an observant copyist? As with many such problems no one overall solution can be given; each case must be judged on its merits. At Luke 1:78 the manuscripts are strong on both sides, the Majority Text plus Sinaiticus and Alexandrinus read the past tense.

John 7:31. NRSV prints as its translation 'When the Messiah comes will he do more signs than this man has done?' but shows the alternative tense 'is doing'. The present tense seems to have been substituted by scribes who felt that the past tense could contradict the fact that Jesus was still performing miracles. See the comparable substitution of one tense for another at John 10:18: 'No one takes it [my life] from me . . .' and 'No one has taken . . .'.

John 14:17 reads '. . . he remains with you and will be with you'.

The first verb there can be understood as present or future depending on the way in which we print the accent in the Greek verb (accents were not written in the earliest manuscripts) but the second verb is in the present tense in some manuscripts and the future in others. The variant can be resolved only after assessing the likeliest sense required in the context. At Galatians 6:2 the change in tense noted in GNB ('you will obey' and the command 'obey') is the difference of one vowel in Greek. Again, the context has to be determinative in resolving this variant.

John 8:57. GNB records the variants: '. . . you have seen Abraham?' and '. . . has Abraham seen you?' (Both could be translated as a statement.) In Greek the difference between 'you have seen' and 'he has seen' is slight. (The name 'Abraham' does not decline and one cannot tell if it is subject or object.) 'Have you seen Abraham?' is the more difficult reading. Is it therefore the original? Abraham is the subject of the verbs of seeing in the preceding verse. Has the author maintained that subject in verse 57, or is it the scribes who have been influenced by that verse? For a full discussion we again suggest consulting commentaries, because it is the overall context that is determinative in variants of this sort.

John 9:4. When Jesus is speaking to his disciples does he say 'I must carry on the work of him who sent me' or 'We must carry on . . .' with the final pronoun being either 'me' again or (with some manuscripts) 'us'? Various combinations and permutations of pronouns can be created out of the confused manuscript evidence, but our question is: What is the likeliest original text written by John? The manuscript support is finely balanced, so critics who look to external evidence do not find an easy solution here. The phrase 'who sent us' is not found elsewhere in John and that fact might make us plump for 'me' at the end of the sentence, but we could again invoke the proviso of our preceding paragraph: namely, must we expect an author to be 100 per cent consistent in his ideas and expressions? In any case, even if we agree that 'me' is likelier than 'us' at the end and that 'us' was introduced by scribes only in those texts that already had 'we' at the beginning, that does not help us to decide if 'I' or 'we' is original there. A full discussion of the variant would require an examination of Johannine Christology and an investigation of comparable speeches elsewhere.

Acts 11:11. GNB and REB print '. . . the house where I was staying' but they note the variant '. . . the house where we were staying'. In

Greek the difference is slight, *ēmēn* with both vowels long 'I was' or *ēmĕn* with the second 'e' short 'we were'. Either could have been written for the other. Thus, this variant could be dismissed as a minor orthographical variant or a spelling slip, but if the change was intentional we need to ask why it was effected, and, more important, which reading is original. What did the author intend? The more difficult reading is 'we'. 'I' appears in verse 5 and that may have encouraged the change to the first person singular.

Acts 13:33. Is the original text 'What God promised our ancestors he would do he has now done for us who are their children . . .' (which looks like a conflate reading) or '. . . done for our children'. REB notes these variants but the text it prints '. . . for the children . . .' is a pure conjecture lacking any manuscript support. There are however two other variants in the manuscripts: '. . . for their children . . .' and '. . . for us, the children . . .'. This latter is what is expected in the context, but that may have been why it was introduced. 'Our children' is the most difficult of the readings, and for that reason should perhaps be considered the original. That would then be the cause of the different attempts to ameliorate the sense.

C) *Christological and Theological Variants*

Obviously, many variants in all categories are theological in the broadest sense, but here we are concerned with Christological and/or theological titles, because this was a comparatively common and obvious area in which the faithful could express their beliefs. Many variants involve the substitution of one divine title for another. Again, a full discussion of the issues involved in any one variation unit must take not only the total context into consideration, but also the scribal proclivities of particular manuscripts. Some manuscripts were more open to the influence of lectionary conventions or liturgical practice: if such characteristics are detected, then, in these instances, such a manuscript is unlikely to represent the original text. (In this respect therefore Hort's advice that knowledge of manuscripts must precede an assessment of readings holds true.)

In looking at these variants, it is worth remembering that in the Greek manuscript tradition most divine names (such as God, Lord, Jesus, Christ) and related names (such as 'heaven', 'Jerusalem', etc.) were commonly abbreviated. Some of them were reduced to only two letters, usually the first and last letter in the name, thus the writing of 'Jesus' instead of 'Lord' or vice versa meant a slight orthographical change.

The following is a selection of such variants noted in the footnotes of the English editions:

John 4:1:	Lord/Jesus
John 6:69:	The Holy One of God/Christ/Christ the Holy One of God/Christ the Son of God/The Son of God/Christ the Son of the living God
1 Corinthians 10:9:	Lord/Christ/God
Colossians 2:2:	Christ/God/God who is Christ/God Christ/ God who is in Christ/God the Father of Christ/God and Father of Christ/God and Father and Christ
Jude 4:	Master and Lord/Master (and) God and Lord/God and Lord
Jude 5:	Jesus/God Christ/Lord/God

Each of these, and others like them, needs to be resolved separately, but it is worth remembering that the word 'Lord' was often ambiguous, sometimes referring to Jesus, sometimes to God. Where the context is not clear, it could well be that scribes would avoid 'Lord', preferring to specify either Jesus or God. Following this line of reasoning, 'Lord' would be original. On the other hand, 'Lord' may be seen as a liturgical improvement on the simple name 'Jesus'. If so, 'Jesus' would be the original reading.

'Master' (not one of the conventional 'divine names') in Jude 4 is ambiguous, used of God and of Jesus, hence it is likely to be original here and the variants are attempts to avoid the ambiguity. The complexity of the manuscript tradition at John 6:69 is characteristic of the relative freedom which the church allowed itself with divine titles. In this instance 'the Holy One of God' seems likely to be original. In 1 Corinthians 10:9 behind the reading 'Christ' is the belief that Jesus himself was operative even in OT times. That belief, prevalent in the early centuries, may account for the change from 'Lord' to 'Christ'. The more difficult reading in Colossians 2:2 is the one which equates Jesus with God ('. . . the mystery of God Christ'). If that is original one can see why there is a plethora of variants intended to prevent the equation Jesus = God, an identification that was often avoided by the church.

The apparent reluctance of the church to equate Jesus and God has affected the textual tradition of virtually all doctrinally sensitive passages in the NT. Among the passages where the identification of Jesus with God seems to have been intended, several are open to differing interpretation and punctuation. These include John 1:1; 17:3; Romans 9:5; 2 Thessalonians 1:12; Titus 2:13; 2 Peter 1:1; James 1:1 (and cf. Matthew 1:32; Hebrews 1:8). At other places there are serious textual disruptions: John 1:18; Acts 20:28; Galatians 2:20; 1 Timothy 3:16; 1 John 5:20.

1 Timothy 3:16 is discussed below under F. Some of the passages concerning punctuation are discussed further below. John 1:18 and Acts 20:28 are discussed now in some detail.

First John 1:18. Do we read 'the only-begotten God', or 'the only-begotten Son'? Many of the modern versions prefer 'God', although other translations are less than clear here. Does the Prologue refer to Jesus as 'God' or 'Son'? 'God' is clearly the more difficult reading stylistically (because 'God' appears earlier in the sentence) and theologically, because of the abhorrence that would have been felt in some quarters at describing Jesus as the only-begotten God. Although some scholars see 'God' as a scribal alteration intended to enhance the Christological standing of Jesus, it is more likely that offence felt by others would have encouraged a change away from an original 'God' to the less offensive Christology implied by the substitution of the word 'Son'.

[Cf. John 1:34. Does John the Baptist proclaim Jesus 'God's Son' or 'God's Chosen One'? REB and other versions draw our attention to the choice to be made, although more variants exist, including 'the Chosen Son of God' which looks like a conflate reading (where two variants have been fused into one). The fact that 'Son of God' is common and 'Chosen One of God' rare suggests that the direction of change seems to be from the original 'Chosen One' to the commonplace 'Son'.]

Now to Acts 20:28. Most English editions mention the major variants here. They are: 'Be shepherds of the church of God (*or* church of the Lord), which he made his own . . . *either a*) . . . through the blood of his Son *or b*) . . . through his own blood.' As far as the variants 'God' and 'Lord' are concerned, the ambiguous title 'Lord' is likely to be original and to have been substituted by 'God' to give us the phrase 'the church of God', common in Paul's writings. That variant is related to the textual problem following. If 'God' were original, a scribe might have hesitated to speak of God having blood, and thus may have been tempted to alter 'his own' to 'his Son', but if he read 'Lord' and took it to mean 'Jesus' then the following 'his own blood' would not cause a problem. The word order in Greek that has 'blood of his own' need not imply a meaning different from the word order 'his own blood'. Both sequences exist in the manuscripts, but the former *could* mean 'blood of his own (Son)'. This absolute use of the adjective 'his own' to mean in effect 'his own Son' is not found elsewhere in the NT. The context seems to require that the Lord (God) obtained the church by shedding his own blood while incarnate. If this is right we have another equation of Jesus and God in a textually uncertain passage.

Now to other variants appropriate to this section.

Matthew 24:36. 'But about that day and hour no one knows, neither the angels in heaven [nor the Son] but only the Father.' Modern editions usually include the bracketed words. These words are absent from the Majority Text and the *Textus Receptus*. AV omits them. It is interesting to observe that the phrase was of such crucial importance that one corrector of Codex Sinaiticus deleted the words from the original and an even later corrector restored the words. The shorter form is likely to be a secondary alteration in order to avoid a reading that casts doubt on Jesus' omniscience. The longer reading is symptomatic of several 'human' or lower Christological ideas that later generations removed. The same variation is to be found in the parallel (Mark 13:32).

Mark 1:1. We noted earlier the textual problem at the end of Mark's Gospel. Now we ask: How did Mark begin his Gospel? Did he say Jesus was the 'Son of God' or not? The words 'Son of God' are absent from the first hand of Sinaiticus and a few other witnesses. Some exegetes have noted that Mark is concerned to show Jesus as the long-awaited Messiah (and he is proclaimed as such by Peter halfway through the Gospel). Moreover, Mark stresses Jesus is the Son of God (and is proclaimed as such by the Gentile centurion at the foot of the cross near the end of the second half of the Gospel – a confession different from that of Luke's centurion). It is possible that the omission was accidental, six of the seven words in the longer text of Mark 1:1 end with the same Greek letter, thereby enabling a careless copyist's eye to jump over two words. However, such a scribe would have had to be remarkably lax at the start of a new book in copying what is in effect its title. The addition of the words could, of course, be explained as a later, pious expansion of a divine title. Perhaps 'The beginning of the Gospel of Jesus Christ' was felt to be too brief and in need of clarification, especially for the benefit of Gentile readers. On balance, we suggest that the longer text is secondary, and, despite its antiquity, the reading should be expunged from our texts and relegated to the footnotes as an example of how the church changed the text of the exemplars they were reproducing. They made such changes because to them these texts were living witnesses, not fossilized documents.

Mark 6:3. Variants here have Jesus 'the carpenter, the son of Mary' or Jesus 'Son of the carpenter and of Mary'. The original reading is likely to be the one that speaks of the carpenter as Jesus' father, as in Matthew's parallel. (Matthew's wording is not exactly the same as this variant in Mark, making it unlikely that the Markan reading was due to assimilation to Matthew). Mark's Gospel shows no awareness of the virginal conception, but at a later stage, when this belief was more widespread, the text was adjusted to describe Jesus as the carpenter and thus avoid his being described as Joseph's son. This seemed important even though it meant that Christians were now describing their saviour as a mere artisan. Celsus, the second century critic of Christianity, ridiculed those who put their faith in a carpenter. Origen, answering Celsus, claims no knowledge of any statement in the NT that Jesus was a carpenter. All that proves is that Origen was ignorant of manuscripts containing what we argue is the original text. The readings are noted in REB and NRSV. Comparable variants, not normally noted in modern English versions, occur in Luke 2. It is clear from the NT that the Virgin Birth tradition is restricted primarily to the opening chapters of Matthew and Luke. Outside the nativity scenes there is little interest in or knowledge about Jesus' parents. (See for instance Romans 1:3; Galatians 4:4, where Paul's arguments about the uniqueness of Jesus' birth do not refer to or depend on Jesus' virginal conception.) In the Lukan birth stories there is a series of variants which show how, even in these early chapters, Luke's writing was perceived to be in need of improvement in order to prevent misunderstandings that could have the effect of diminishing the teaching on the virginal conception. At Luke 2:33, 41, 43 most manuscripts speak of Jesus' 'father' and his 'parents', whereas other manuscripts have the secondary 'his mother and Joseph' or the like.

Luke 3:22. In this account of the baptism Codex Bezae (D) has the words derived from Psalm 2:7 'You are my begotten Son' in contrast to the reading of other manuscripts: 'You are my beloved Son in whom I am well pleased'. The Matthaean and Markan parallels to the verse agree with the words 'You are my beloved Son . . .', which could suggest that the text of the bulk of manuscripts of Luke is due to assimilation, but few critics are willing to accept the testimony of manuscript D virtually alone (although there is patristic testimony, and the reading seems to be known in the lost, apocryphal Gospel according to the Hebrews). However, it is worth considering if it is the idea of Jesus' being begotten or that of his being what was sometimes seen as merely an 'adopted' Son that would be the reason for the change within the manuscript tradition of Mark. A full consideration of the issues would need to take into account, among many other things, Luke's teaching about Jesus' baptism and also his use of the OT.

John 3:13: 'No one has ever gone into heaven except the one who came from heaven – the Son of Man.' NIV and other editions give the variant adding the words 'who is in heaven' at the end. Are those words original or merely a later explanatory gloss? If original, here is Jesus claiming to be in heaven while talking to Nicodemus. If that claim caused a problem, one can understand the reason for the omission of the words. This longer reading, which has the support of the Majority Text and all other witnesses except for a few important, early Alexandrian manuscripts (Sinaiticus, Vaticanus, Papyri 66 and 75), is likely to be original; it accords with Johannine theology and its high claims for and by Jesus, the pre-existent Logos.

Galatians 1:6. Does Paul say God called the Galatian Christians 'by grace' or 'by the grace of (Jesus) Christ'? A quick answer would be to favour the shorter text (read by some of the Western manuscripts, together, it would seem, with the fragmentary Papyrus 46) and to explain the alternative as a pious expansion, but many critics hesitate to go wholeheartedly with the Western evidence. JB even omits 'grace' without manuscript support for so doing (unless P[46] can be quoted).

At Philemon 1:14 GNB prints 'message' and notes the variant adding 'of God'. That addition appears in differing positions. There is also a variant adding 'of the Lord'. All of this again suggests that such additions are secondary, pious expansions. NIV shows similar variants at the opening greetings in Colossians 1:2, where manuscripts add the name 'Lord Jesus Christ' at the end of the verse. Also at 1 Thessalonians 1:1 the simple 'Grace and peace to you' has been expanded with 'from God our Father and the Lord Jesus Christ'. NIV also shows the same change to the original text at 2 Thessalonians 1:2.

D) *Proper Names*

This section concerns names other than divine titles, which are dealt with in the preceding section. Quite often changes in the manuscripts that involve a proper name are to be accounted for as the harmonization of parallel passages. But not all can be explained on those grounds. Sometimes the scribe seems to be correcting (as he sees it) factual information.

Matthew 8:28. 'Gadarenes' or 'Gerasenes' or 'Gergesenes'. Most editions refer to these variants. The same variants appear in the parallels to the passage in Mark 5:1 and Luke 8:26, 37, which complicates any attempted resolution of these variants based on scribes' assimilation of parallels. It may well be that Matthew, Mark and Luke each originally had a different name and the various forms known to us are harmonizing readings, but that does not assist our deciding which name belongs to each Gospel. On the basis of superior manuscript attestation most textual critics are satisfied to print 'Gadarenes' in Matthew, 'Gerasenes' in Mark, 'Gerasenes' or, sometimes, 'Gergesenes' in Luke. If the original authors knew their geography of Palestine, then it would be clear to them that neither Gerasa, being thirty miles from the Sea of Galilee, nor Gadara, being five miles away from the lake, would be probable in the story. (It has, however, been suggested that 'Gadara' may mean 'the territory of Gadara' which reached to the lake.) But it is not always evident that the biblical authors' knowledge of geography was exact, and it may have been left to later readers to see the problem and to suggest alternative names. The reading 'Gergesenes' seems to have been coined by Origen and to have entered the manuscript tradition through his advocacy. If that is correct, then we cannot claim 'Gergesenes' as the original text in any of the Gospels.

Matthew 10:3. 'Lebbaeus' or 'Thaddaeus'. Again, editors usually reach a decision on external attestation alone, the eclectic school preferring 'Thaddaeus' with Sinaiticus and Vaticanus. There also exist the readings: 'Thaddaeus called Lebbaeus', and 'Lebbaeus named Thaddaeus'. Those favouring the Majority Text accept the latter, but opponents see this as a conflate reading. In support of arguments for the longer texts one could indicate that both shorter forms are accidental shortenings, whereas there is no obvious reason why a scribe would have altered 'Lebbaeus' to 'Thaddaeus' or vice versa.

Matthew 10:25; 12:24. 'Beelzebul' or 'Beelzebub'. In English we are used to Beelzebub 'The Lord of the flies', thanks to its occurrence in the AV. The same variants are found in the parallels in Mark 3:27 and Luke 11:15. Can we invoke the rule of dissimilarity in order to make two of the parallels differ from the third, and, if we can, which are the preferred readings throughout? Or should we again consider that in this instance the NT knew one form only which was later corrupted? Those accepting the latter procedure note that Beelzebub is basically the form preferred by the Latin tradition, not the Greek. It entered the English through the Vulgate spelling. Although it makes sense as a transliterated Hebrew term, so too does Beelzebul 'Lord of dung'. Beelzebul is to be preferred in a Greek NT and in English renderings of the Greek.

Matthew 15:39. 'Magadan' or 'Magdala' or 'Dalmanutha'. The same variants occur at Mark 8:10, once again prompting the question: If we are here concerned with assimilation of one text to the other, which is the likeliest direction of change? Neither site is known; neither name is attested outside this context. Most editors print 'Magada' or 'Magdala' in Matthew on the basis of the manuscript attestation (Sinaiticus, Vaticanus, Bezae for the former; the majority of manuscripts for the latter), and for similar reasons print 'Dalmanutha' in Mark where Sinaiticus, Alexandrinus and the Majority Text agree against different readings in other witnesses.

Matthew 27:16 and 17. 'Barabbas' or 'Jesus Barabbas'. This is an interesting variant. Although 'Jesus Barabbas' is not well attested in the manuscript tradition, it is found in a few Greek and versional sources. One can readily appreciate scribal reluctance to copy the name 'Jesus' when it belongs to an insurrectionist. Origen thought it improper that a sinner be called Jesus. As a fairly common name, 'Jesus' could well have been Barabbas' personal name, Bar Abbas or Bar Abba his patronymic (cf. Simon Bar Jonah and Joseph Barnabas), but, as Christianity developed, 'Jesus' would obviously be associated primarily with Jesus Christ of Nazareth. Matthew's trial scene shows Pilate confused, being confronted by two men called Jesus. Scribes of this Gospel could have twice deleted the name 'Jesus' prefacing 'Barabbas'. A change in the opposite direction, that is, a scribe *adding* 'Jesus' before 'Barabbas', seems less likely. Palaeographical considerations support the presence of the name 'Jesus': in verse 17 the word preceding 'Jesus' ends with the same letters as the abbreviated form of this name.

Acts 4:6. 'John' or 'Jonathan'. Both John and Alexander in the verse are unknown. 'Jonathan', the reading of Codex Bezae, is likely to be a factual correction, because it was known from Josephus that Jonathan son of Annas was high priest in succession to Caiaphas.

2 Peter 2:15. 'Bosor' or 'Beor'. The former is not a name known elsewhere, but it is the one usually printed as original in 2 Peter because of the strong manuscript support for it. The variant 'Beor' is a name known in the Greek OT and assimilation to the Septuagint probably accounts for its introduction here.

Colossians 4:15. 'Nymphas . . . his house' or 'Nympha . . . her house'. Is this a woman or a man with a house church? The proper name here is spelled the same in Greek for male or female (although the accent differs) but the pronoun is unambiguous – either 'his' or 'her'. (There is another variant, 'their'). The only way to resolve the problem seems to be to make a decision based on one's opinion of the trustworthiness of certain manuscripts. GNB and REB also note the alternatives 'Junia'/'Junias' at Romans 16:7. The difference between the genders in the Greek depends on the accents and, as early manuscripts were written without accents, we have many manuscripts where the text is ambiguous. ('Julia' also exists in the oldest witness, Chester Beatty Papyrus 46 of c. 200, but this could be a scribal slip in view of 'Julia' in verse 15.)

For other variants of this sort noted in the footnotes (particularly in NRSV and RAV) see: Matthew 1:7–8: 'Asa' or 'Asaph'. Does the genealogy refer to the name of a psalmist (Asaph) or to a king of Judah (Asa)? And in which direction is the change likely to have gone? Normally modern editors accept the reading supported by their favourite manuscripts. Defenders of the Majority Text favour 'Asa', the eclectic school 'Asaph'. As in English, so in Greek; there is little difference in the two names, and one may have been written for the other by accident. Cf. Matthew 1:10: 'Amon' or 'Amos'. Are we dealing with a king of Judah or an Amos? Perhaps the two are merely different forms of the same name. Luke 3:32: 'Sala' or 'Salman' ('Salmon') where it is likely that the Lukan form of the name in his genealogy is 'Sala' which was assimilated to 'Salmon' read in the Matthaean parallel. See also Luke 3:33 where names are transmitted in a bewildering variety of spellings, and number: some manuscripts have two names, some three, standing before 'son of Hezron'. If one is editing a text one must do something here, but there seems little agreement among scholars – hence the footnotes in NIV, REB, NRSV and others.

E) *Assimilation*

Many variants occur because of the overwhelming desire to iron out apparent discrepancies in parallel accounts of the same saying or story. As a rule of thumb we suggest that one should accept as original the reading that makes the parallels *dissimilar,* given the tendency to remove differences. But that principle is not a rule of iron to be applied mechanically. A full investigation should also look at the language and style of both or all of the authors of the parallel accounts. It also needs to consider any explanations other than harmonization which could have given rise to variation. But at the end of the day, it is true to say that the vast majority of textual critics find assimilation a powerful force behind many scribal alterations. This is especially true in the Synoptic Gospels – Matthew, Mark and Luke. Those Gospels contain many incidents, sayings and stories in common. The church, by and large, tended to assimilate accounts in Mark and Luke to the Matthaean version. Matthew's was the Gospel most frequently cited by the early Christian writers. His Gospel was the best-known and it did, of course, stand in pride of place in most manuscripts of the Gospels, so it was not surprising that his wording was the one that came to mind when the version in Mark or Luke was being copied.

But that is not the only way assimilation works. As we see in the examples heading the following list, even the text of Matthew was harmonized. Sometimes the harmonization involves addition, sometimes omission, variants in word order, or substitution. Examples are found under those headings earlier in this chapter.

Matthew 5:44: 'Bless those who curse you, do good to those who hurt you.' This addition noted in, among others, NIV is one of several variants in the verse. The addition comes from Luke 6:27–28.

Matthew 11:19: 'Wisdom is vindicated by her ...' Some

manuscripts have 'sons' as the last word, others 'deeds'. 'Sons' comes from Luke 7:35.

Matthew 14:24. Was the boat 'in the middle of the sea' or 'many furlongs away from the land'? Although the latter is echoed in John 6:19, the former is likely to have come from Mark 6:47.

Matthew 19:9. Some manuscripts, including Vaticanus and the bulk of Byzantine witnesses, add 'And the man who marries a woman so divorced commits adultery'. Here the assimilation is to the earlier occurrence of this teaching in Matthew 5:32.

Matthew 20:16. Some manuscripts add at the end 'Many are called but few are chosen'. This longer text is likely to come from Matthew 22:14, where these words conclude another parable.

Matthew 20:22. Some manuscripts add at the end of Jesus' question: 'or to be baptized with the baptism that I am baptized with?'. The same manuscripts add in verse 23 (after 'To drink my cup') 'or to be baptized with the baptism with which I am baptized'. The additions seem to have come from Mark 10:38 and 39 respectively.

Mark 2:22. The words 'But new wine is for new wineskins' are not firmly established in the text. Codex Bezae and the Old Latin witnesses omit them. It is possible that they are not original to Mark, but were introduced from the parallel in Luke 5:38.

Mark 7:24: '. . . Tyre [and Sidon].' The longer text is from Matthew 15:21.

Mark 7:28: '[Yes], Lord'. The longer text is from Matthew 15:21.

Mark 14:65: 'Prophesy! [Who hit you?]'. The disputed words occur in Matthew 26:68 and Luke 22:64. Did the later evangelists find these words in Mark? (Most scholars working on the literary interdependence of the Synoptic Gospels argue that Matthew and Luke used Mark's Gospel.) If one does accept that argument then the omission of the disputed words by certain manuscripts has to be accounted for as a careless scribal error. If the argument is that the words were added by scribes of Mark through assimilation to the parallels, then the text resulting from that decision has to be taken into account by scholars working on the Synoptic Problem, accounting for the relative order of these Gospels and explaining the reasons for the similarities and dissimilarities between them. That is because what will have been printed are three parallels where Matthew and Luke agree *against* Mark. These so-called Minor Agreements, allegedly occurring coincidentally in Matthew and

Luke, need to be taken into account by those who argue that Matthew and Luke were working independently on Mark.

Luke 6:10: 'He said [angrily] . . .' The addition is from Mark 3:5.

Luke 23:38: 'There was an inscription over him [written in Greek and Latin and Hebrew] . . .' The longer text is a rare instance of borrowing from the Johannine parallel (John 19:20).

F) *Greek*

Even though our concern in this book is with variants that are found in the footnotes of the English versions, it is clear that many variants we have already encountered exist only because of special peculiarities in the Greek language. The variants in this section are gathered here because the reason for their existence is something distinctive in Greek. Some are very important.

For example, Romans 5:1, where many editions alert us to the variants 'we have peace' and 'let us have peace'. Was Paul so confident in the changed status of Christians that he could tell the Romans they already have peace (i.e. with God), or was he encouraging them to create the conditions of peace? The statement 'we have' and the hortatory 'let us have' are remarkably similar in appearance and sound in Greek. It is the difference between *echomen* with either the short letter 'o' (omicron) or the long 'o' (omega). Phonetically, the change could have occurred in either direction. On balance, it would seem that Paul's confident 'we have peace' was not shared by later readers and scribes, who thus made the verb hortatory to encourage Christians in their own day. 'We exult' or 'let us exult' in verses 2 and 3 are due to the same type of changes in the Greek. (cf. also 1 Corinthians 15:49: '. . . we will wear the likeness of the heavenly man' or '. . . let us wear . . .')

At Romans 14:19 there is a similar dilemma, not easily resolved, between manuscripts that have the equivalent of 'we pursue' following the statements in the preceding two verses, or the equivalent of 'let us pursue' initiating the exhortations that are to be found in verse 20. Also see Hebrews 6:3 'we will do' or 'let us do' noted in NRSV where the same differences occur in the manuscripts. Another omicron–omega change is at 1 Corinthians 15:49: Did Paul write that 'we shall bear the image of the man from heaven' or was the passage hortatory (as many textual critics accept, despite the relative paucity of witnesses for this form), namely 'let us bear . . .'?

Mark 1:4. GNB prints 'John appeared in the desert baptizing and preaching . . .' but notes in the margin that some manuscripts read 'John the Baptist appeared in the desert preaching'. There are several variants in the verse but these two renderings hinge on the presence or absence of the word 'the' in Greek, and all other variations follow from this. If 'the' is original, Mark is calling John 'the baptizing one' i.e. the Baptist (and there is evidence elsewhere that this was his normal way of describing John). If there is no 'the', 'baptizing' is a verb parallel to 'preaching' later in the verse, and both verbs are probably dependent on the verb translated above as 'appeared'. The co-authors of this monograph agree on the translation ('*was* preaching' in preference to '*appeared* . . . preaching'), but disagree about the variant 'baptizing' or 'the Baptist'. I. A. Moir preferred 'John was baptizing and preaching'; J. K. Elliott prefers 'John the Baptizer was preaching'.

Luke 2:14. In the Gloria do the angels speak of '. . . peace among those whom he favours' or '. . . peace, good will among men'? Only one Greek letter makes the difference – the presence or absence of the letter 's' (sigma) – between the invocation to all for peace and good will and the more restrictive request for peace for a particular group. In matters like this is it appropriate to look at the manuscripts in support of each reading, or is such a concern less relevant here? Codex Vaticanus and Codex Sinaiticus contain both readings: correctors altered 'of his good will' of the first hand (that is, the original scribes' writing) to 'good will'. Despite the direction of the change visible in those two manuscripts the alteration in the opposite direction is more likely. 'Men whom God favours' is a phrase with counterparts in the Dead Sea Scrolls: it is perhaps the more difficult reading and one which scribes with the minimum of alteration could adjust.

John 3:25. REB prints 'John's disciples were engaged with some Jews about purification' noting the alternative 'a Jew'. NRSV has 'Now a discussion arose about purification between John's disciples and a Jew' and notes the variant that some ancient authorities read 'the Jews'. Which is original? On the face of it 'a Jew' seems the more difficult and therefore the reading more likely to be corrected: 'the Jews' are regularly the opponents of Christ's message in the Fourth Gospel. Two letters in Greek make the difference. In Codex Sinaiticus the original plural was altered in the manuscript itself by a corrector to the singular. Of the early papyri that contain this verse the Bodmer Papyrus 75 of the early third century has the singular whereas Papyrus 66 of c. 200 has the plural. Thus both readings have ancient testimony.

John 10:29. GNB, NIV, REB, NRSV and others alert us to the variants that result in the alternatives that may be translated 'That which my Father has given me is greater than all' and 'My Father who has given them to me is greater than all'. Not surprisingly much has been written in commentaries and elsewhere about these distinctions. They are weighty issues indeed but they go back to the Greek manuscripts, some of which have *ho* (neuter: 'that which') whereas others read *hos* (masculine: 'he who') and the matching comparative adjective 'greater' (neuter *meizon* with short 'o', and masculine *meizon* with the long 'o'). All these apparently small changes have a significant effect on the meaning of the text. There are other variants here which concern word order and omissions. These are not reflected in the footnotes in the English versions, but they too are symptomatic of the problems in the verse. One often finds in the variation units with greatest theological or interpretative importance that there is a complicated textual tradition as scribes tried to unravel, and in some cases further ravel, the problems. Again, having grasped the text-critical problem we need to turn to modern commentaries and grammars. In this verse the editors of the United Bible Societies' Greek testament print, without confidence, the neuter pronoun and the neuter form of 'greater'.

1 Corinthians 2:4: 'My speech and my proclamation were not with plausible words of wisdom . . .' This verse throws up at least a dozen fascinating variants, one of which occurs in the footnotes of NRSV, namely, '. . . were not with persuasiveness of wisdom . . .' The NAV has '. . . with persuasive words of human wisdom . . .' and a note referring to the variant omitting 'human'. Much of the difficulty hinges on whether one Greek letter appears twice or once. (The readings with 'human' are secondary; the word is likely to have been added as an explanatory gloss.) The issue we are more concerned with is the Greek word *peithois*. In many manuscripts it precedes the word meaning 'of wisdom' (*sophias*) and the problem is that the adjective from which *peithois* comes is not known in the whole of Greek literature. If it were coined by Paul, it requires a noun, hence the presence of 'words'. However the 's' (sigma) at the end of *peithois* could have arisen through dittography, i.e. the accidental

doubling of the 's' at the beginning of *sophias*. *Peithoi,* from the noun meaning 'persuasiveness', does exist. It looks as if this is the original text but that problems began once the doubling of the 's' caused confusion that lasted over several generations of copying.

1 Corinthians 13:3. Did Paul say that even if he gave his body to be burned and did not possess love he would gain nothing by it, or did he say '. . . give my body that I may boast . . .'? The two verbs in Greek, 'to boast' and 'to be burned', differ in this verse by only one letter. As in other comparable cases, the change could have occurred in either direction. Also, as in comparable cases, where an orthographical change could have been easily effected, it is probably less relevant to adopt as original a reading based on the evidence of particular manuscripts. 'To be burned' is the more difficult reading, although as a piece of rhetorical exaggeration it is admirably suited to the context; it could have been deliberately altered if it was believed that Paul did not die by burning. The alternative 'to boast' is fairly common as a phrase in Paul. Had he written it here, a deliberate change away from this is less likely.

1 Thessalonians 2:7. Does Paul claim that we were 'like very young children' or 'gentle' when 'we were with you'? This variant, included in GNB, is due to the similarity in the Greek for the word 'children' (*nepioi*) and 'gentle' (*epioi*). Did the letter 'n' occur in the original? As the word preceding ends with 'n' are we here to consider an accidental dittography or a misreading that resulted in *nepioi*, or is the opposite the case, namely haplography – two letters 'n' reduced to one in copying, thus resulting in *epioi*? Paul often calls his converts 'young children', but not himself. However, the word 'gentle' occurs only once elsewhere in the whole of the Greek Bible (2 Timothy 2:24). The context of motherhood makes 'babes' more likely to be the original, although the idea of 'gentleness' is also appropriate in the context. Stalemate?

1 Timothy 3:16. Much ink has been spilt on the variants here, and this verse is often used as a touchstone by radical defenders of the Majority Text, the *Textus Receptus* and the AV. The issue concerns the beginning of verse 16, which is a verse that many commentators – and translators – take as Paul's quotation from an early Christian hymn. Did the quotation begin with the relative pronoun 'who' (presumably, in its original context, meaning Jesus) or the neuter relative pronoun 'which' referring to the Greek neuter noun in the preceding verse 'mystery'? Or did it begin with the name 'God'? All

these in Greek are similar in appearance – especially when, as was normal, the name 'God' was abbreviated to the first letter (theta) and the last (sigma). We thus have a choice between *ho, hos* and *ths*. Accident could explain each of them as secondary to the others. The neuter '(the mystery) which was revealed in the flesh' is possible but less likely to be original when compared with the alternatives. The change to the neuter would have occurred when a scribe copying from a manuscript that had *hos* 'who' altered the pronoun to agree with the neuter noun immediately preceding. Such a change reflects more a concern with grammar than content, since the credal hymn clearly refers to Christ. (Obviously the early manuscripts did not separate the second half of verse 16 in the way most modern editions do, printing it in poetic form.) Of the other readings, perhaps an original 'who' was changed to 'God' once it was felt that the meaning of the original poetic context needed explication. Another reason for the deliberate change from 'who' to 'God' is that the church may have wished here to emphasize its belief in the divinity of Jesus. (It is interesting to see how the comparatively rare statements in the NT which equate Jesus and God are subject to textual variation or to ambiguities as we have seen earlier in this chapter). Four of the earliest manuscripts that read 'God' (including Sinaiticus and Claromontanus) do so as corrections of an original 'who'. In other words 'God' was the preferred reading of a later generation and the change in those manuscripts was no mere accidental misreading. It seems that 'who' is the text to print. If so, this credal hymn conforms with the others in the NT (Philemon 2:6ff. and Colossians 1:15ff.), which also commence with a relative pronoun.

Hebrews 12:1: '. . . the sin that all too readily restricts us . . .' or '. . . distracts us . . .' REB notes this variant, which depends on a minor change involving two letters in Greek. The reading translated 'distracts' occurs in the oldest witness, Chester Beatty Papyrus 46 (c. 200), and some scholars have defended the originality of this text.

1 John 2:20: 'All of you have knowledge' or 'You know all things'. This is another difficult variant to resolve. Again, commentators and exegetes need to be concerned to explain a variant that depends on the difference between the Greek *panta* ('all things') and *pantes* ('all people').

Revelation 12:18. Who stood on the shore, the dragon or the

seer? The manuscripts divide. GNB includes this variant, which depends on the presence or absence of a final 'n'. Do we read, with some manuscripts, *estathe* ('he stood' i.e. the beast of verse 17) or *estathen* ('I stood' i.e. the subject of the verse following)? The way in which one resolves the problem will have repercussions for the punctuation of the paragraphs.

G) *Variants Requiring Specialist Attention*

Our subdivision of the variants is arbitrary and several variants could belong in a different category or in more than one category. That is certainly true of the hodgepodge of variants noted here as requiring specialist treatment or as being of specialist interest.

One particularly problematic section concerns the parable of the two sons in Matthew 21:28–32 which seems to have been transmitted in at least three forms. These are largely contradictory. Which son said 'Yes', which one said 'No', and which son did the will of the father? Answers to these questions will differ, depending on which version of the parable is read. The resolution of the problems lies outside the scope of this book. Readers who wish to progress further into textual criticism of this complexity are advised to consult the books recommended in the Postscript. One of the textbooks listed (that by Aland and Aland) devotes several pages of detailed discussion to this parable.

Another baffling variant is at Acts 16:13. REB prints '. . . where we thought there would be a place of prayer' and notes as a variant reading '. . . where there was a recognised place of prayer . . .' Metzger's *Textual Commentary* is a suitable point of departure when discussing problematic verses, although in this instance he is able to report only that the 'least unsatisfactory solution' is 'where we thought there was a place of prayer'. (For another obscure passage that has created a whole array of variants see James 1:17, especially the words translated in REB as 'With him there is no variation, no play of passing shadows'.)

Hebrews 11:11. GNB prints 'It was faith that made Abraham able to become a father even though he was too old and Sarah herself could not have children. He trusted God . . .' and has in the footnotes: 'Some manuscripts have: "It was faith that made Sarah herself able to conceive even though she was too old to have children. She trusted God . . ." ' (cf. NIV, NRSV). REB's text has the verse refer to Sarah. It may be that the reference to Sarah was an explanatory gloss that found its way into the text thus creating the variants required to make her, and not Abraham, the subject of the whole sentence. There are linguistic and lexicographical problems in addition to the transmissional problems in accepting the originality of the text translated in GNB.

Many text-critical variants are still unresolved and there is much debate about several problem verses. Textual criticism is by no means a closed or completed area of study.

H) *Word Order*

Manuscripts often vary in the sequence of words in a sentence. Often changes in word order in Greek do not make much difference, if any, to the sense and are not relevant to translators. However, there are instances when changes in word order in the Greek can be displayed in a modern version. GNB and REB show us that the order of the words 'in my name' at John 16:23 is crucial to the interpretation. Are the hearers to ask for anything they wish in Jesus' name, or are they to be granted their wish in his name? See also Luke 8:27. NRSV: The demoniac had been *naked for a long time* (the reading with the external evidence generally favoured by most textual critics). There is a variant telling us that the man had been *demon-possessed for a long time*. The manuscripts differ in their position of the words translated 'for a long time'. At Luke 18:11 did the self-righteous Pharisee '*stand by himself* and pray' (the more difficult reading) or did he 'stand apart and *pray to himself*'?

I) *Punctuation*

Punctuation variants are of crucial importance for exegesis and for translation. The United Bible Societies' *Greek New Testament* has a special critical apparatus giving details of various levels of punctuation variants. But these are not text-critical variants as commonly understood, and we shall not get involved with them in this book. Our earliest manuscripts did not use marks of punctuation in any consistent or obvious way. So, although some discussion about punctuation allows an appeal to the manuscripts, it is impossible to use manuscript evidence alone when deciding on the punctuation of the NT in modern editing. Among passages of crucial importance are John 1:3–4; 7:38; Romans 9:5; 1 Corinthians 7:34 (although text-critical considerations of word order are involved here); Ephesians 4:12; Titus 2:13. Discussion of these passages is to be found in good commentaries. We shall concern ourselves here only with Matthew 11:9 where NRSV is aware of the alternatives 'Who did you go out to see? A prophet?' and the different punctuation 'Why did you go out? To see a prophet?' (The last sentence could be read as a statement in answer to the question.) This is admittedly largely a matter of punctuation as the Greek interrogative can be either 'why?' or 'what?', but there are textual variants regarding the position of the verb 'to see' before or after 'prophet'. If 'to see' is after 'prophet' this makes unambiguous the translation 'To see a prophet', but that reading could be a later attempt to specify a preferred interpretative meaning over another. Verses 7 and 8 have a similar ambiguity concerning punctuation, with the verb 'to see' going either with the preceding question or with the following question (or statement).

5

Textual Criticism: Past, Present and Future

The Past

Textual criticism of the NT is not a new process. It is almost as old as the texts themselves. As we saw in Chapter 3, the African church Father, Tertullian, castigated Marcion (died c. 160) to the extent of six books for interfering with the Gospel text. Marcion had tried to solve the problem of Gospel variations by scrapping all but Luke which he edited to accord with his own views on various subjects. Another solution of the variations in the Gospels was worked out by Tatian, an Assyrian who flourished about 160 AD. He produced a 'scissors and paste' life of Christ from the four Gospels in a way which shows that these four were already well established at the time he wrote. His work, known as the Diatessaron (that is '(one created) from four'), was widely used in the Syriac-speaking churches until the fifth century AD. This work is of interest from the text-critical point of view because it contains many unusual variations from the common text and it has been found that some of these readings have made their way to Western Europe and are reflected in medieval harmonies of the Gospels in languages such as Dutch and English.

Origen (185–254 AD), who lived in Alexandria and later moved to Caesarea, complained in his commentary on Matthew about the differences in manuscripts that had arisen on account of the carelessness or the audacity of scribes. He showed considerable interest in textual problems, as too did Jerome (342–420 AD), who also was alert to textual variation in the manuscripts to which he had access.

For several hundred years through the medieval period Greek was largely unknown in the West. It was through the Latin translations that the Bible reached Britain. From time to time various authors, including Bede, attempted to produce popular English versions for those who knew no Latin, and it was from the

Latin that the first major English version was made – that of John Wycliffe (1330–84) or of his pupils, Nicholas of Hereford and John Purvey. This very literal work suffered from the fact that its authors were regarded as heretical and indeed their work was officially condemned at the Council of Oxford (1407), and further translations were forbidden. In spite of this, the translation continued to be used and prepared the way for the new developments which resulted from the work of Erasmus in the early sixteenth century.

An additional factor that had begun to make itself felt was the invention of printing, which spread from the middle of the fifteenth century. In theory this meant the production of standard copies, though it must be said that the limited amount of type available in early days meant that the type was often distributed and reset for different parts of a book, so that reprints and reissues of the same book often varied considerably from the previous printing. Nevertheless, the way was opened for the standard printed text which could be relied on more than manuscript copies as a means of stabilizing the text. Printing not only rendered scribes largely redundant but it encouraged scholars to set about editing texts on a more scientific and reliable basis. Printing also halted the progressive scribal corruption of texts and in part even reversed the process.

Erasmus' NT in Greek was printed in 1516 along with a Latin translation. This publication gave encouragement to the work of Tyndale and others. (A further influence on textual criticism was the 1522 German NT translation of Martin Luther.) Erasmus did not print any variant readings. A greater interest in variation of the text was aroused by the publication in 1521/2 of the famous Complutensian Polyglot. The fifth volume of this work contains the text of the NT in Greek and Latin with a series of key numberings to assist in relating the Greek to the corresponding Latin. Both the Complutensian and the text of Erasmus influenced the editorial work of Theodore Beza and of Stephanus (or Robert Estienne) at Paris. Stephanus' third edition of 1550 became the standard for subsequent editors for three hundred years. Because of his interest in producing a concordance of the scriptures, he introduced the modern verse system in his fourth edition of 1551. Stephanus' texts derive from Erasmus and represent the late manuscripts employed by him. Although other Greek texts were available, they were, on the whole, ignored by editors or not available to them. Stephanus himself included in his marginal notes the variants of a dozen or so manuscripts.

The need for standardization of the Greek text was encouraged by the fixing of the Latin Bible as the Vulgate edition of 1590 revised in 1592. The Dutch printers, Bonaventura Elzevir and his nephew, Abraham, published the second edition of their Greek NT in 1633 with the claim that it gave the text that was 'received by everyone'. The Elzevirs' edition is thus the *Textus Receptus* proper.

Not everyone was happy with this situation and various attempts were made in subsequent centuries to improve the Greek testament. Constant attempts were also being made in the sixteenth and seventeenth centuries to better the state of the English translations. The two endeavours go more or less hand in hand.

In 1627 King Charles I received from the Patriarch of Constantinople the famous Codex Alexandrinus (A 02) and thirty years after this some of the readings of that manuscript were included by Brian Walton in his famous Polyglot. This was financed by Cromwell and did much to stimulate study of the text of the Bible. The NT volume had evidence also from Codex Bezae (D 05) and Codex Claromontanus (D 06), but of even more value than the critical apparatus was the appearance on each page of the Greek NT of two Latin versions, together with Syriac, Ethiopic, Arabic and Persian, and a literal Latin rendering of these versions. It was obvious from comparisons that there was a good deal of variety, and further study of the problem was stimulated. In addition, the sixth volume contained a critical apparatus providing even further evidence for examination.

In an endeavour to improve the situation John Fell, Bishop of Oxford, produced in 1675 an edition of the Greek NT with the evidence of additional manuscripts. He made use of a hundred Greek manuscripts and also referred to versions, including the Gothic. Perhaps his main claim to fame was his encouragement of John Mill. Mill's work took a long time to come to light, for he lost his financial support when Fell died in 1686, and it was 1707 before the edition was published in Oxford. For the versions Mill was dependent on Latin translations produced by others. But he expressed quite a number of opinions on the value of individual manuscripts and on various critical problems in his *Prolegomena,* which was written after his edition of the text had been completed.

Alarm was caused in the Church of England by this work, which indicated over 30,000 variant readings in the text. More than one of the radical opponents of Christianity claimed that nobody need any longer pay attention to the scripture because of its unreliability.

Mill's work was taken seriously by Edward Wells who published between 1709 and 1719 a new critical edition of the Greek NT, which had the honour of being the first critical text not based on the *Textus Receptus.* Attention was at last being focused on the earlier manuscripts, though readers were slow to appreciate their evidence and their significance. In this tradition Richard Bentley tried to supplant the TR as did Daniel Mace. Other eighteenth-century British textual scholars included William Bowyer and Edward Harwood.

The spotlight now turns to the continent where Johann A. Bengel, born in Tübingen in 1687, grew up in an atmosphere favourable to the critical study of the NT. As a student and subsequently as a pastor, Bengel was interested in the variant readings of the NT text and aimed at publishing a new and correct edition. Bengel made numerous collations of manuscripts and in 1725 published his *Prodromus.* He took advantage of the work of Mill and others and in 1734 produced his edition of the Greek NT. Bengel stuck to the *Textus Receptus*, but he used his margin to indicate readings which he thought were genuine and he added an apparatus as an appendix to throw further light on various readings which he considered important enough to mention.

In the world of textual critics Bengel is famous for three things. 1) He made a practice in his apparatus of giving the evidence both for and against particular readings. 2) He produced a series of criteria for assessing various readings, among which was the very important dictum that the more difficult reading is to be preferred to the easier one. The easier reading would be seen to be an amelioration, correction or gloss on the more difficult one in a situation which would not operate the other way round. 3) Bengel began the practice of dividing manuscripts up into families according to the readings of their text.

We turn next to another continental scholar, Johann J. Wettstein, a Swiss Protestant native of Basle, who became a Professor in Amsterdam. He was also associated with a publishing house in the same city and it was through this work that he became interested in the NT text. In spite of his severe criticisms of Bengel, Wettstein followed him in the practice of printing the TR and putting other preferred readings at the foot of the text. It was shortly after Mill's work had been published that Wettstein produced in 1713 a treatise on variant readings in the NT, and this was followed by his *Prolegomena* to the text in 1730 and finally by his two-volume folio edition of the Greek NT in 1751–2. In his *Prolegomena* Wettstein gave a mass of detail about the manuscripts, versions and Fathers and improved the apparatus of former editors by introducing the system of using letters for the uncial manuscripts and numerals for the minuscules. This system was a considerable saving of space over the contractions used by Mill.

One aspect of the system was that the letter system was used for each group of books independently and this was a source of much confusion. For example, 'D', stood for Codex Bezae in the Gospels and Acts but for Codex Claromontanus in the Pauline epistles. Furthermore a manuscript containing several parts of the NT canon was allocated a different number in each section. This system was modernized and improved by C. R. Gregory in 1908 and is still used today.

Wettstein was one of the first to look beyond the Greek text and to consider the evidence of the versions and the Fathers, though he was somewhat inconsistent in rejecting the old manuscripts but using their agreement with the versions to establish the 'true' readings. He recognized also one of the important issues with regard to the text of the Fathers, namely that their quotations from scripture have often been harmonized with the biblical texts in general use.

It fell to Johann J. Griesbach, Professor of New Testament at Jena from 1775 till his death in 1812, to try and create some order in the wilderness. In the matter of grouping manuscripts Griesbach took the division a stage further. Originally positing five or six groups he laid emphasis on three which he called Alexandrian, Western and Byzantine. Alexandria he associated with the name of its great biblical scholar, Origen; a Western Group was headed by Codex Bezae and a third area group derived from the other two and was associated with Constantinople. The leading representative of the Alexandrian group was Codex Alexandrinus (A 02).

Griesbach's main editions were his first in 1775–7, the second in 1796–1806 and the third produced in 1803–7. This third edition was reprinted in London in 1809 and 1818. In addition, Griesbach produced sundry studies of the problems of textual criticism. For the first time in Germany a scholar ventured to abandon the TR at many places and to print the text of the NT in the form to which his investigations had brought him. This text stimulated much interest and was widely republished in Britain and America and formed the basis of numerous continental editions. The extent of publication shows the interest in the Greek NT at that time, and it also encouraged others to search out Greek manuscripts and to seek further evidence from the versions and the Fathers.

Griesbach also recognized another problem for the textual critic – 'mixture'. This intermingling of text-types is so wide-spread that most texts can be said to show some evidence of it. It was also clear to Griesbach that many manuscripts do not exhibit a text which follows the evidence of one family text, but show traces of readings from two or more families. Griesbach also recognized a further important feature, namely that a manuscript may belong to different groups in different areas of its text. The codex A 02 has a different type of text in the Gospels, in Acts and the Catholic Epistles, and in Paul.

At about this time two considerable additions were made to our knowledge of manuscripts by Johann M. A. Scholz, at Bonn University, who is said to have increased the lists of known manuscripts by some 600 items, and by C. F. Matthaei, who became a professor in Moscow, and who collated a large number of manuscripts there and elsewhere and published his results in a twelve-volume edition of the Greek NT (Riga, 1782–8).

Several other minor editions were produced in the meantime which all added their quota of manuscript knowledge to the list, but the next outstanding name in the history of the text is that of Karl Lachmann (1793–1851). As he was a distinguished philologist and textual critic in other fields, he decided to try his hand at the NT and to apply to it the same principles that he had applied in dealing with classical and other literature. Lachmann, accordingly, sent an article in 1830 to one of the leading German theological periodicals in which he outlined his views, and then several months later he published his text. This had no preface, but only a few appended notes explaining his activities. As Lachmann was the first to abandon the TR entirely, this in itself alarmed critics, but there were many complaints also about the printing of the *Prolegomena* only in a periodical. The result was that Lachmann's new views were declared by many to be a waste of time and he waited nearly ten years till the storm died down before publishing his second edition (1842–50) with a more adequate preface.

Basically Lachmann saw himself as producing from ancient authorities the text of the NT as it was available in the time of Jerome at the end of the fourth century. With this in mind he was prepared to discard the bulk of later material and also to ignore the notion of 'families' of manuscripts put forward by Griesbach and others. When we consider that Codex Sinaiticus was not yet discovered and that B 03 was only partially edited, it meant that Lachmann had a very restricted number of manuscripts available. In cases where some of his main witnesses were defective, he was dependent on only one or two manuscripts. This narrow choice was also a target for criticism. Lachmann also saw his text 'not as a final text, but simply as a sure historical basis for further operations of internal criticism, which might lead us in some cases nearer to the primitive text'. One main effect of this was that he went behind previously printed texts (as indeed his principles compelled him to do) since most of them reflected the work of Erasmus in 1516, which in turn reflected the text of the later manuscripts that Lachmann had decided to put aside.

A younger contemporary of Lachmann followed up his work and some of his ideas. This was Friedrich Constantin von Tischendorf (1815–74). He was appointed to a chair of Theology in Leipzig at the age of 28 and spent the greater part of his life touring Europe and the Middle East in search of manuscripts, collating some of those already known and discovering a great many others – chief of which was the Codex Sinaiticus (01), on which he worked at Sinai and Cairo. He eventually persuaded the Orthodox monks who owned it to send it to the Tsar of Russia as a present. After this he made a detailed study of it and produced two editions of its text, one of which was made in a special typeface in imitation of the fourth century characters, in which the original was written.

In all, Tischendorf produced some eight editions of the Greek NT. Of these, four are important as records of new textual material being incorporated into the text. His last, a two-volume work completed in 1872, is still a standard work, since no proper replacement of it has yet been achieved, even though much more material has become available in the intervening century. Tischendorf died in 1874 and the *Prolegomena* for his work was completed by C. R. Gregory in 1894. Tischendorf looked for other support for unusual Greek readings (e.g. Latin or other versional evidence). He rejected for his text what he regarded as transcriptional errors and variants which arose from harmonization of parallels. He also indicated a preference for variants from which others could be explained as developments and, like Griesbach, he was interested in the grammatical usage of the NT writers. Tischendorf's monumental eighth edition of the Greek NT (which differs from the seventh of 1859 in over 3,000 places and shows a return to the witness of the older manuscripts) is still a mine of useful information. The apparatus to this work has considerable complications and requires practice in the use of it. (See Plate 7.) Help can be found in C. R. Gregory's *Prolegomena* and the subject is also dealt with by A. T. Robertson in his *Introduction to the Textual Criticism of the New Testament*, where Chapter 4 is entitled 'The Use of Tischendorf'.

The name of Samuel Prideaux Tregelles (1813–75) ought to be mentioned at this point. This self-taught textual critic collated many manuscripts in the British Isles and on the Continent, where he collaborated with Tischendorf. He also produced an edition of the Greek NT along lines similar to, albeit independently of, the approach of Lachmann. That is, his edition is based on the oldest manuscripts available to him. It was perhaps the work of Tregelles, as much as anyone else, that paved the way for the edition of Westcott and Hort and for the preparation of the 1881 Revised Version of the New Testament.

By the time Tregelles died churchmen in England, and particularly those associated with the Convocation of Canterbury, had already turned towards the idea of producing a revision of the Authorized Version. Naturally this raised the interesting question about which Greek text should be used for the translation, and voices were heard in favour of retaining the traditional Greek text of the NT. Chief among the champions were F. H. A. Scrivener, Vicar of Hendon, and J. W. Burgon, Dean of Chichester. Scrivener expounded his views in a number of publications, but more particularly in his *Introduction to the Criticism of the New Testament*, published in 1861 with a fourth revised posthumous edition edited by his friend, E. Miller (Oxford 1894). He also produced in 1875 a volume entitled *Six Lectures on the Text of the New Testament and the Ancient Manuscripts which contain it, Chiefly Addressed to those who do not read Greek.* Burgon's diatribes on the other hand were published in various newspaper and periodical articles and only later were they gathered into book form. The best-known is probably that entitled *The Revision Revised,* where Burgon let loose a torrent of abuse on the ancient manuscripts. There has recently been a revival of interest in Burgon, especially in his argument that because there was no control over the text in the early centuries all sorts of corruptions crept in, which it took hundreds of years for the church to expel – in other words, the further back one went the *more* corrupt the text seems to be.

Perhaps the criticism was all the more bitter because Westcott and Hort had already made their new Greek NT text available privately to the Revision Company and so, in the eyes of Scrivener, who was one of the conservative members of the Company, they had taken an unfair advantage of their position. Opposition or no, B. F. Westcott, Regius Professor of Divinity in Cambridge and his colleague, F. J. A. Hort, Hulsean Professor, produced in the same year as the Revised Version (1881) their two volumes entitled *The New Testament in the Original Greek.* The first volume of this work, which remained standard in Britain for over fifty years, contained the text, while the second was in the form of a lengthy Introduction giving an account of Westcott and Hort's theory and a discussion of individual readings.

Most of the nineteenth-century textual critics were primarily concerned with obtaining better knowledge of the manuscript sources, but Westcott and Hort seem to have felt that most of the necessary work had been done in that direction and they concentrated on using the work of others to produce the best text they could make. In the main they followed the lines laid down by Lachmann, but they held that most of the important variants were in existence earlier than the fourth century, certainly in the third and perhaps even in the second century. This observation has to some extent been confirmed by recent papyrus discoveries. Like Lachmann, and much to the annoyance of Scrivener and Burgon, they were prepared to ignore the bulk of the later manuscripts and to use what they considered the direct ancient tradition to be found in Codex Vaticanus (B 02), which they preferred to Codex Sinaiticus. They also tried to take further the notion of dividing manuscripts into families which stem from a common ancestor and are identifiable by certain readings which they share. However, they recognized that, while family groupings were possible, many of the manuscripts in the course of copying had gone through a process of cross-fertilization giving rise to 'mixed' or 'conflate' texts.

Westcott and Hort, in the tradition of Bengel, Griesbach and Lachmann, reached the conclusion that the true text may be found in a small number of older manuscripts to the neglect of the large stock of later material. They devised or adapted various rules and applied them to the material available to them. They then expressed the view that readings should not be considered in isolation. From individual readings they therefore turned to individual documents and considered their general behaviour and reliability in other readings, and so built up a general picture which could be used to illuminate the passage in question. From such a general picture one may be able to establish that the scribe of a particular manuscript was very careless or that another was a poor speller. Such considerations may cause quite a reduction in the number of readings to be seriously considered at any one point in the text.

By the time all the documents had been examined it became apparent that some of them have a close relationship and this led to a consideration of what Westcott and Hort call 'Internal Evidence of Groups'. Here they formulated a rule which reads 'Community of reading implies community of origin'. From this two lines of development are possible for the critic. Firstly if XX and YY both exhibit a common reading, it may be possible to deduce from them the reading of their common ancestor, ZZ, and, secondly, it may be possible to set up some form of genealogical tree to establish the relationship of this group of manuscripts to other groups. In practice, however, they turned to certain, preferred manuscripts when they attempted the actual construction of a text. It is the belief that certain manuscripts or a group of manuscripts are to be relied upon that influenced most textual critics over the following century. In practice this meant pride of place was given to Vaticanus (B 02) and to Sinaiticus (01), which they together called the Neutral Text. They rejected most of the distinctive readings of the Western text-type, of the polished Alexandrian manuscripts (C 03, 33 and others) and of the conflated Syrian (that is Byzantine) text-type (A 02 and the bulk of later cursives).

The only major figure comparable to Westcott and Hort and Tischendorf is Hermann Freiherr von Soden (1852–1914), who made extensive collations, especially of cursive manuscripts. He produced a distinctive Greek NT in 1913. His is a difficult apparatus to consult because of his own unique sigla and nomenclature for the manuscripts. The new system of sigla reflects his theories about the history of the text. The text itself is seldom referred to, but his apparatus, for all its difficulties and blemishes, still gives evidence and readings not easily found elsewhere. (See Plate 8.)

The main edition that has dominated the scene during the twentieth century has been the Nestle text. This edition of the Greek NT was first published in 1898. At its inception it was a compromise edition that printed the text read by at least two out of three other texts (from its third edition the texts of Westcott and Hort, Tischendorf, and Weiss). From the seventeenth to twenty-fifth editions this strict principle was watered down. The Nestle text is now in its twenty-seventh edition (see Plate 10). It adopted for its twenty-sixth and present edition the text prepared by the United Bible Societies. This is an eclectic text, which, although leaning heavily on Westcott and Hort, nevertheless prints on occasion readings without the support of Vaticanus and its allies. Some critics of the UBS/Nestle edition have encouraged its committee to create an even more rigorously eclectic text. Meanwhile, editions of the Majority Text and even reprints of the *Textus Receptus* have been published.

In some ways the last seventy years or so have seen a less confident approach to text-critical theories. A well-known American scholar, Eldon J. Epp, has dubbed this the 'twentieth-century interlude' in textual criticism. Nevertheless since Westcott and Hort's and von Soden's day much has happened. For one thing manuscripts even older than Sinaiticus and Vaticanus have come to light, in particular the spectacular early papyri. The text of other manuscripts already discovered has been published and analysed.

In fact, it is the discoveries of texts earlier than the great uncials, on which Westcott and Hort built their elaborate theories of text-types, that has caused the breakdown of previously accepted theories. There has thus been a weakening in the 'cult of the best manuscripts' in favour of an appraisal of a wider selection of witnesses.

The twentieth century has also been characterized by several developments. There have been attempts to present as comprehensively as possible the findings of recent discoveries.

Scholars have also tried to bring order to the mass of evidence available to the critic. The important work of establishing new and better editions of the versional evidence as well as promoting better editions of the Fathers has also been gathering pace.

Eldon J. Epp's chapter 'Textual Criticism' in the volume *The New Testament and its Modern Interpreters* (edited by Eldon J. Epp and George W. MacRae) is a useful survey of the work in the field done in the past fifty years. The volume is one of three under the series title *The Bible and its Modern Interpreters* published to celebrate the centenary of the American Society of Biblical Literature. (The volume was published by Scholars' Press, Atlanta, Georgia in 1989.)

Our own concluding section looks at work currently under way that will produce fruits in the coming decades.

Present and Future

New Testament textual criticism is by no means a dead or deserted subject. At the present there are several enterprises at work on aspects of the discipline.

The bulk of work in the field is initiated by the Institute for New Testament Textual Research at the University of Münster in Germany, to which we have referred in earlier chapters. This Institute was founded by Kurt Aland (whose vigour and energy lie behind numerous enterprises and publications, most notably the Nestle Greek testament). The Institute is now directed by his widow, Barbara Aland. The team of researchers there has been responsible for publishing a vast range of texts and tools. The resources of the Institute are used for creating, maintaining and updating the critical apparatus of both the UBS *Greek New Testament* and the Nestle edition. Under the auspices of the Institute, Greek, Greek–English and Greek–German Synopsis texts have been published. Among the tools, they have published an exhaustive concordance to the NT and also a computer concordance. Another responsibility of the Institute is the maintenance of the official register of all NT Greek manuscripts. It possesses microfilms of virtually all Greek NT manuscripts. Also the Institute publishes valuable monographs and studies in its series *Arbeiten zur neutestamentlichen Textforschung* (Studies in New Testament Textual Research). The Institute is also active in the field of Coptic and Syriac NT manuscript studies. The long-term goal of its researchers is to produce a major critical edition of the NT comparable to Tischendorf's eighth edition. This

'New Tischendorf' is being actively pursued, and preliminary work has already started with the Catholic Epistles.

The Christian University in Abilene, Texas is working on the manuscripts of Acts under the direction of Carroll Osburn. He is currently assembling an exhaustive critical apparatus. There are plans afoot to publish at least some of this work, possibly in conjunction with the Münster Institute.

The International Greek New Testament Project comprises two committees, one in North America, the other in Great Britain. Together they are currently responsible for directing work on a full apparatus to the Fourth Gospel, which might well be published in electronic form in instalments, as well as, ultimately, in conventional book format. As a preparation for that full apparatus, a volume has just been published containing the evidence of the papyri: these fragmentary witnesses are problematic to display easily in a normal apparatus, which is why their peculiar problems are being dealt with in this separate volume. The committees published a two-volume apparatus to Luke in 1984–7 which is the fullest assembly of Greek, versional and patristic testimony to that Gospel available. The apparatus to John will be a successor to those volumes.

The *Centre Jean Duplacy* headed by Christian-Bernard Amphoux is the main NT text-critical body in France. It is named after the renowned critic Jean Duplacy, who did so much to keep the subject alive in France in the 50s, 60s and 70s. One of the current plans under way there is the preparation of the textual history of Mark's Gospel. The aim of the project is the production of a multi-volume series showing the manuscript history not only in Greek but in most of the versions as well. The volume on the Greek is designed to show how the text of the principal text-types, Western, Alexandrian, etc. developed.

For many years the Vetus Latina Institute based in Beuron in Germany has been working on the Latin Bible with the aim of uncovering the forms of Latin independent of Jerome's revision, and the Vulgate, and presenting the full range of pre-Jerome texts and Latin patristic citations. The work of that Institute has resulted in a series of monographs and an ongoing series of text volumes which will eventually cover the whole Bible. Several instalments on the New Testament text have appeared.

In the earlier part of this book we have referred to the existence of a Majority Text Society in the USA. Members of that body are fighting a rearguard action to defend the *Textus Receptus* and by extension the KJV. Its output is often polemical and directed against modern Greek editions, and translations based on these. Many of the active members of the Society are alert to current text-critical debates and recent publications. The very existence of such a ginger group is a sign of the wider importance attached to the results of textual criticism.

Individual academics and groups of scholars are busy on different aspects of the versions, even the more obscure ones like the Ethiopic. Learned articles, monographs and even newly published texts and editions appear from time to time. The bi-monthly Australian journal *New Testament Textual Research Update* succeeds in keeping a wider public informed on these and other developments. There is even a monthly journal in Japanese *Studia Textus Novi Testamenti* that has been appearing since 1966 with related publications on the text of Mark, Matthew, and the NT papyri.

Many of the ambitious plans for work on the New Testament text require the energies and manpower of teams of researchers. Nevertheless there are many scholars, mainly professional academics but a few gifted amateurs, who devote most of their scholarly activities to aspects of the NT text. The Society of Biblical Literature's annual conference in the USA attracts large numbers to its text-critical seminars. The international learned society, *Studiorum Novi Testamenti Societas* (SNTS), has for many years maintained a lively text-critical seminar in its annual programme. Publications resulting from all these activities are found in several theological journals and in the lists of major academic publishing houses. Some of the more recent titles appear in the list of books for further reading at the end of this book.

Postscript

In this section are gathered three topics about which there is general interest: the use of computers in textual criticism, the likelihood of spectacular new finds of manuscripts, and the place of conjectural emendations to the NT text.

Computers

Inevitably in a field like textual criticism, in which a large mass of evidence is available, computers and electronic data processing have begun to make their impact. The reading of a manuscript is still a human activity – scanners are unlikely to be able to cope with the individual script and handwriting of each and every manuscript. However, once a manuscript has been read by human eyes then its distinctive readings can be, and in some research programmes are already being, entered into an electronic database. From that base readers can draw on any preferred selection of manuscripts or types of variant. This storage and retrieval method can be used to facilitate comparisons between manuscripts and assist or create new collations against any available electronic text. Computers will enable a critical apparatus to be assembled in which text-critical witnesses can be displayed in whatever degree of complexity is required. Likewise, a unit of variation of any length can be devised using the database.

Once the distinctive readings of a manuscript are recorded by its collation against a base text then a computer program can reproduce the distinctive text of that manuscript in its entirety. This means that the collation of any two, or larger groups of, manuscripts can be compared electronically with one another. Family relationships and textual allies may be sought using such information. The Institute for New Testament Textual Research at the University of Münster has already made some preliminary investigations into manuscript interrelationships. Much more is to be done in this area.

Another use of computers is in locating tiny manuscript fragments in their context. Small scraps of newly discovered manuscripts are often difficult to place, particularly when no words are preserved in their entirety and concordances are therefore useless. Sometimes, a text may not prove to be literary and that is the end of the matter, but if it is suspected that a small fragment could conceivably have come from the NT, a computer can be used to check if the surviving combinations of letters in the manuscript could have come from a NT book. Computer searches have already been undertaken with great success; some new biblical fragments have thereby been identified, while other allegedly biblical manuscripts have been rejected.

[Some readers may have heard of the argument proposed by the Catalan textual critic, Josep O'Callaghan, which claims that one of the Dead Sea Scrolls is a fragment from Mark's Gospel. The novelty of the suggestion that a Christian text is to be found so early in Qumran has fascinated many scholars. Such an identification is acceptable only with over-imaginative reconstructions that include a peculiar spelling and an unlikely deciphering of damaged letters. Computers have been brought in recently to show that the surviving letters legible on this fragment are only possibly a part of Mark if certain letters, inconvenient to the identification with Mark, are reinterpreted to conform to it. More significantly, other searches have tried to show that the fragment could be from the Greek OT. All of this confirms the earlier suspicions of many scholars who doubt if the fragment comes from a biblical text at all.]

Will We Find More Manuscripts and Do We Need More?

Further extensive worldwide searches for NT manuscripts in libraries and other collections are unlikely to be made. All the obvious places have already been systematically visited, particularly in the 1950s and 1960s. Possibly, some long lost manuscripts may be discovered in Eastern Europe but the large increase in the numbers of registered manuscripts recorded in the last fifty years is unlikely to be seen again. St Catherine's Monastery on Mount Sinai yielded up a dozen new NT Greek manuscripts and hundreds of other religious texts in several languages in the mid–1970s. These await official publication but from what is known of the biblical texts there are few surprises in store. Archaeologists, however, are still turning up new finds of NT manuscripts, especially in Egypt, and it is to be expected that the number of papyrus fragments will increase. Of course, it still remains a possibility that some spectacular finds may be made, although the raising of the water table by the new high dam at Aswan is bound to diminish the possibility. There is always excitement at each new discovery, especially if the manuscript is an old one or one that contains a good proportion of its original text.

In many ways we already have more sources than we can readily handle. NT textual criticism in one sense is not dependent on new manuscripts. It is the case that new discoveries seldom produce genuinely new readings, that is, readings never previously recorded, so we are unlikely to find many useful and interesting new variants. But there are readings which sometimes present themselves as likely to be the original which have been dismissed as such by many critics because they are not found in many witnesses. As more manuscripts are discovered and as an increasing number of manuscripts are read, it may well be that a reading once weakly attested is seen to have wider support and thus may be more favourably looked upon. Similarly, a reading known only in late witnesses may be found to have early support. (This has frequently happened: several Byzantine readings have in the past twenty years or so been found to be supported in early papyrus texts.) So the search for new manuscripts goes on, and the collating of manuscripts already known proceeds apace. Those whose interests lie in investigating the interrelationships of manuscripts are also concerned to find as many missing links in the Greek textual tradition as they can. For such research every manuscript could theoretically be the missing jigsaw piece required to assist in the construction of a family relationship.

Conjectures

The overriding presumption and presupposition of NT textual criticism is that the original reading has survived somewhere in the tradition – obviously not in any one manuscript or in one group of manuscripts. But it is assumed that by a process of detection the original can be recovered from some of the manuscripts. In the classics and in OT textual criticism such assumptions are not possible. There is sometimes too little evidence, too few or too late manuscripts for us always to be able to reconstruct their text with confidence. With the NT the position could hardly be more different. Not only do we have many manuscripts and many manuscripts of an early date but recent scholarly attempts to edit the NT text are done with a confidence that the original text is there to be discovered in the manuscripts. Sometimes editors reach different conclusions, sometimes an editorial judgement is questionable, but behind the debate the assumption is that the manuscripts, supported or supplemented by the versions and by quotations in the writings of the Fathers, will yield the original text.

And yet there is sometimes the suspicion that occasionally, perhaps only once or twice in the whole of the NT, all the witnesses have been corrupted and that the original reading has disappeared for ever. If such a suspicion is entertained then the next logical step is to try to guess what the original might have been. Nineteenth-century scholars had great fun with conjectural emendations of the NT. Some rewritings were very ingenious – some too ingenious. The footnotes to the Nestle texts show us, almost for the sake of historical novelty, some of these nineteenth-century conjectures. Some modern exegetes and commentators still hazard guesses as to what the original author meant to write when they find the printed text problematic. At 1 Corinthians 4:6 the sentence is difficult to understand. NIV has '. . . so that you may learn from us the meaning of the saying, "Do not go beyond what is written"'. The Greek here literally means '. . . so that you may learn from us to think not beyond what is written' or 'that you may learn in our case the meaning of "not above what is written"'. As a result, more than one exegete has suggested that the passage is corrupt, and that what seems to have happened is that a marginal note was accidentally incorporated into the text causing a nonsense reading. But not only is the difficult text found in every single manuscript read to date but (as is usual in such matters) the conjectures never achieved universal acclaim.

Conjecture in any literature should only be the last resort – it should be appealed to only when it is clear that no sense whatsoever can be found by modern readers in any of the documentary sources. Conjecture often turns out to be a mere imaginative rewriting.

One place where a good case has been made out for a conjectural reading is at 1 Corinthians 14:34–35. These verses are found in all known witnesses; they contain the command enjoining women to remain silent in church, a sentiment uncomfortable for many readers. However, it has been shown that these words seem to contradict Paul's own teaching earlier in the epistle. In 11:5, 13 he seems to encourage women to teach. Some of the language of the disputed verses is at variance with Pauline usage elsewhere, particularly in the way he appeals to the Law here without citing the text. But more important than this, from the text-critical point of view some of the manuscripts seem to indicate that the words were looked upon with suspicion in antiquity. Codex Vaticanus marks the verses with two dots and a dash, a symbol that occurs twenty seven times in that manuscript, nearly always in passages where the text is suspect. There is evidence in some other texts, most strikingly in the Harklean Syriac Version or in Origen's *Hexapla*, that scribes did resort to such symbols to draw attention to passages they knew to be of textual interest. Certain other manuscripts have the verses in chapter 14 indented, or written as a distinct paragraph on their own. Also, the verses appear in some manuscripts in a different place, i.e. after verse 40. As we have seen in Chapter 4, when a text appears in different positions in the manuscript tradition its originality is often questionable.

So, perhaps in the case of the verses conventionally numbered 1 Corinthians 14:34–35, the words may have merely been a marginal gloss written up out of 1 Timothy 2:11–15 and deliberately incorporated into 1 Corinthians at a later date. If we do then decide to jettison these verses from Paul, we must be aware we are doing so without any Greek manuscript support at all. We are rewriting the NT, emending the text by using guesswork.

Another conjecture that has had a fair amount of attention is at John 19:29 where *hyssopos* (hyssop) does not seem to be the right word. Hyssop is a small bushy plant, hardly suited for lifting a sponge to the lips of Jesus on the cross. Some success has attended the conjectural emendation *hyssos*, which means 'javelin'. In this instance the conjecture has been supported by a couple of late manuscripts, but this was either a careless contraction of the longer word, or reflects a scribe's conjectural emendation. If we do not wish to accept the conjecture, we must try, as most commentators do, to explain the symbolic significance of hyssop in the story.

Some other places where conjectures have been suggested now follow:

Luke 24:32. The word 'burning' caused problems to copyists and translators. Various conjectural emendations have been made, not just by modern exegetes but by scribes and translators, and these include 'heavy', 'veiled', 'blinded', 'hardened', and 'terrified'.

At Acts 2:9 one finds in commentaries and in learned articles attempts to adjust the list of place names. That is because in the list 'Judean' (firmly established in the manuscripts) seems wrong; it is grammatically and geographically out of place. Hence conjectures have been offered. These have seldom met with universal approval, and it still behoves the reader to make sense of the text as transmitted in the manuscripts or at least to admit that the author was inaccurate.

Acts 12:25. The reading that many text critics prefer on external evidence is 'to' Jerusalem, but there are variants reading 'from', 'out of'. All readings have stylistic and other problems against their originality. The context requires Paul and Barnabas to be leaving Jerusalem. Westcott and Hort suspected a primitive error here that affected all the manuscript tradition. If that opinion is accepted, then the way is open for conjectural emendation.

At Acts 16:12 the Nestle-Aland and UBS testaments print in the text a conjecture that may be translated 'A city of the first district of Macedonia' (i.e. a city in the first of the four districts into which Macedonia was divided). If with the manuscripts one reads the text that means 'The first city of the district of Macedonia' we are confronted by the inaccuracy of the statement and the inappropriate meaning of the word 'district'. But, rather than resort to conjecture, one might prefer once again to doubt the accuracy of the original author's statement in this instance.

2 Peter 3:10. GNB gives us several alternatives for the last verb in the verse: 'vanish', 'be found', 'be burnt up', 'be found destroyed'. Others exist. Metzger's *Commentary* confesses that none of the available readings seems to be original. This leaves the door open for wholesale emendation and many suggestions have been forthcoming, as can be seen in good commentaries.

***

There are two rules to be borne in mind if one is tempted to emend the text:

1) The proposed emendation must possess transcriptional probability and explain how the copyist (or author) came to err.

2) The conjecture must be intrinsically probable, that is it must be something the original author is capable of having written, suiting his style and theology. These two conditions must be fulfilled if anyone other than the mere guesser himself is to be satisfied and confident with the result. And then the conjecture can be allowed to stand only if no good arguments are produced to prove the conjecture mistaken. The number of conjectures that meet the criteria will be small, but these would then merit attention.

Bibliography

Books for further reading: The suggestions on this list are books published or reissued since 1984. Each is concerned with the Greek text, but there is much in all of them that can be of benefit to readers without knowledge of Greek.

B. Aland and J. Delobel (eds), *New Testament Textual Criticism and Church History: A Discussion of Methods* (Kampen: Kok Pharos, 1994) (= *Contributions to Biblical Exegesis and Theology* 7)

K. Aland and B. Aland, *The Text of the New Testament* (Grand Rapids: Eerdmans, and Leiden: Brill, 2nd English edition, 1989)

D. A. Black, *New Testament Textual Criticism: A Concise Guide* (Grand Rapids: Baker, 1994)

B. D. Ehrman, *The Orthodox Corruption of Scripture: The Effect of Early Christological Controversies on the Text of the New Testament* (New York and Oxford: Oxford University Press, 1993)

B. D. Ehrman and M. W. Holmes (eds), *The Text of the New Testament in Contemporary Research: Essays on the* Status Quaestionis (Grand Rapids: Eerdmans, 1995) (= *Studies and Documents* 46)

J. K. Elliott, *Essays and Studies in New Testament Textual Criticism* (Cordova: el Almendro, 1992) (= *Estudios de Filología Neotestamentaria* 3)

J. K. Elliott (ed.), *The Principles and Practice of New Testament Textual Criticism: Collected Essays of G. D. Kilpatrick* (Leuven: Leuven University Press and Peeters, 1990) (= *Bibliotheca Ephemeridium Theologicarum Lovaniensum* 96)

E. J. Epp and G. D. Fee, *Studies in the Theory and Method of New Testament Textual Criticism* (Grand Rapids: Eerdmans, 1993) (= *Studies and Documents* 45)

B. M. Metzger, *The Text of the New Testament: Its Transmission, Corruption, and Restoration* (New York and Oxford: Oxford University Press, 3rd edition, 1992)

B. M. Metzger, *A Textual Commentary on the Greek New Testament* (London and New York: United Bible Societies, 2nd edition, 1994)

D. C. Parker, *Codex Bezae: An Early Christian Manuscript and its Text* (Cambridge: Cambridge University Press, 1992)

W. A. Strange, *The Problem of the Text of Acts* (Cambridge: Cambridge University Press, 1992) (= *SNTS Monograph Series* 71)

H. A. Sturz, *The Byzantine Text-Type and New Testament Textual Criticism* (Nashville, Camden and New York: Nelson, 1984)

L. Vaganay and C - B. Amphoux, *An Introduction to New Testament Textual Criticism* (Cambridge: Cambridge University Press, 1991)

***

Editions of the Greek New Testament currently available:

United Bible Societies, *Greek New Testament* (Stuttgart: Deutsche Bibelgesellschaft, 4th edition, 1993)

Nestle-Aland, *Novum Testamentum Graece* (Stuttgart: Deutsche Bibelgesellschaft, 27th edition, 1993) [Nestle-Aland adopted the text of the UBS edition.]

Z. C. Hodges and A. L. Farstad, *The Greek New Testament According to the Majority Text* (Nashville, Camden and New York: Nelson, 2nd edition, 1985)

The New Testament: The Greek Text Underlying the English Authorised Version of 1611 (London: Trinitarian Bible Society, 1976) [This is a modern edition of the *Textus Receptus.*]

Appendix

A Short Glossary of Technical Terms

APPARATUS CRITICUS – A shorthand system to indicate variants and their sources printed below or alongside a printed text.

AUTOGRAPH – The original author's manuscript in his own handwriting, from which is produced the ARCHETYPE. The archetype is the text written out by a professional scribe and the form in which the work was published. All copies derive from this.

CANON – Literally a 'measuring rod'. Refers to the list of books regarded by the church as composing its scriptures. 'Canonical' therefore means 'having the status of scripture' or 'included in the canon'.

CODEX – Leaf-form of book. Superseded the roll-form.

COMMENTARY – Extended explanation of a text.

CONFLATION – The combining of two existing readings to produce a third. At John 9:8, for example, some manuscripts say 'he was blind', some 'he was a beggar', while some have 'he was a blind beggar'. This third reading could be described as having combined the text of the other two, and is hence a conflate text.

CURSIVE or MINUSCULE – Lower case script in which certain individual letters of a word are joined and words normally separated from one another.

DITTOGRAPHY – See below under HAPLOGRAPHY.

DOXOLOGY – An ascription of glory to God. Often poetic in form.

EDITION – A New Testament in the form of a printed book. More accurately this should be referred to as a printed edition.

EXEGESIS – The art of explaining the text by means of a commentary intended to describe the author's meaning.

EXEMPLAR – The manuscript from which a copy is transcribed.

101

FATHER – A theological writer or commentator of the early church. Most Fathers wrote in Greek or Latin; a few in Syriac.

GLOSS – A (marginal) explanation of, or commentary on, a difficult or unusual word.

HAPLOGRAPHY – Writing only once what should be written twice. In practice one often has to weigh this scribal mistake against the opposite phenomenon DITTOGRAPHY, i.e. writing the same thing twice.

HARMONIZATION – An attempt by scribes, usually unconsciously but possibly also deliberately, to assimilate the passage being copied to a close parallel elsewhere. This is a frequent cause of change in the Gospels where parallels, especially within the Synoptic Gospels (Matthew, Mark, Luke) are sometimes close but not exactly the same. There was a tendency to make these parallels agree. Other examples of harmonization occur when the text was assimilated to its immediate context or even to a more remote context in the same book. Harmonizations also occur between the OT citations in the NT and the OT itself.

HOMOEOTELEUTON – The accidental shortening of a word or phrase facilitated by similar spelling at the end of two of the words. For uncials written in continuous script, the recurrent letters need not, of course, occur only at the ends of words and, to be precise, such an optical error is better called PARABLEPSIS (literally 'looking askance') or LIPOGRAPHY (meaning the accidental omission of letters because the scribe's eye has jumped over several letters or words in the EXEMPLAR).

ITACISM – The levelling of vowels to an 'i' sound. This sometimes affected spelling and may account for variants such as at John 19:41 an 'empty' tomb or a 'new' tomb – the word 'new' in Greek (*kainon*) and the word 'empty' (*kenon*) are similar in appearance and sound (cf. Galatians 2:8 'new' deceit or 'empty' deceit, or 2 Peter 2:4 'chains (*seirais*) of darkness' or 'pits (*sirois*) of darkness').

LEMMA – see under PATRISTIC TESTIMONY

LOGOS – Used as a divine title for Jesus in the Johannine writings and in patristic texts. It refers particularly to Jesus' existence prior to the incarnation.

MAJORITY TEXT – See under TEXTUS RECEPTUS

ORTHOGRAPHY – Conventional or correct spelling.

PALIMPSEST – A parchment manuscript which has been rubbed over again (Greek *palin* = 'again' + *psao* = 'I rub') to obliterate the original script and thus allow reuse of the manuscript.

PAPYRUS – Vegetable product, obtained mostly in the Nile Valley, consisting of sheets made from the fibrous pith of the papyrus plant by pressing together two layers of strips at right angles to each other.

PARCHMENT or VELLUM – Animal hide rubbed with pumice in preparation to take writing.

PATRISTIC TESTIMONY – Passage of the New Testament found in the work of a Father either as a LEMMA (verse or phrase set off separately) to be commented on, or as a quotation within the author's text illustrating his argument.

POLYGLOT – A Bible containing the text in a number of languages. The six volume Complutensian Polyglot of 1522 contains the OT in Hebrew, Latin and Greek, and the NT in Greek and Latin. Walton's Polyglot of 1655–7, also in six volumes, includes the NT in five languages – Greek, Latin, Syriac, Ethiopic, Arabic (as well as Persian for the Gospels).

READING – The actual words found in a manuscript for the verse or phrase being considered.

RECTO – Commonly used to refer to the side of a papyrus page on which the fibres are horizontal. Sometimes 'recto' means the right hand page of an open codex.

ROLL or SCROLL – Book made of sheets of papyrus or parchment glued together in a row designed for rolling up.

SCRIPTORIUM – The room in a monastery set apart for scribes to copy manuscripts.

SEPTUAGINT – The most influential of the Greek versions of the OT traditionally said to have been written by seventy (or seventy-two) translators, hence the name *septuaginta* ('seventy'). The name is often written in Roman numerals (LXX).

SIGLA – The signs, symbols, letters, numbers and other abbreviations found in a critical apparatus to refer to the textual witnesses. (Singular = siglum.)

STEMMA – The pedigree of manuscripts shown in a genealogy or family-tree.

TEXTUS RECEPTUS
OR
RECEIVED TEXT – The Greek text of the NT which was the usual printed edition up to the end of the nineteenth century. Technically it refers to the 1633 edition of the Elzevirs' Greek testament, which claimed to be the 'text received' by everyone. The name is more loosely applied to the MAJORITY TEXT, i.e. the bulk of Byzantine, medieval manuscripts.

UNCIAL – Writing in single, upper case, letters usually without separation of words. Sometimes called MAJUSCULE.

VARIANT (READING) – One of a range of available readings at a given point.

VERSION – A NT text in a language other than the Greek, e.g. Old Syriac Version or English Authorized Version. (PRIMARY VERSION – A version made by direct translation from the Greek, e.g. Latin. SECONDARY VERSION – A version made from a primary version and not direct from the Greek, e.g. Persian.) N.B. An ancient version is not by definition necessarily an ancient manuscript.

VERSO – Commonly used to refer to the side of a papyrus page on which the fibres are vertical. Sometimes 'verso' means the left hand page of an open codex.

VULGATE – The common description of the version of the Latin Bible associated with the translation of Jerome (342–420 AD).

WITNESS – A manuscript, version or Father whose text is the authority for a particular reading.

Indexes

Index of Themes and Proper Names

Index of Biblical References

The following passages are discussed in Chapter 4:

1 Corinthians	
2:1	52
2:4	71
7:34	76
10:9	59
13:3	72
15:49	69
15:51	52
15:54	40, 41

2 Corinthians	
1:11	55
8:7	55
11:3	47

Galatians	
1:6	63
2:5	50
2:20	60
6:2	57

Ephesians	
1:1	49
4:12	76

Philippians	
1:14	63
3:13	54

Colossians	
1:2	63–4
1:7	55
2:2	59
2:13	55
3:4	55
4:15	66

1 Thessalonians	
1:1	64
2:7	72
3:2	52

2 Thessalonians	
1:2	64
1:12	60

1 Timothy	
3:16	72–3

Titus	
2:13	60, 76

Hebrews	
1:8	60
2:9	53
6:3	69
11:11	74–5
12:1	73

James	
1:1	60
1:17	74
2:20	53

1 Peter	
2:21	53
3:18	53
4:1	53
5:2	50

2 Peter	
1:1	60
2:13	53
2:15	66

1 John	
1:4	55
2:20	73
5:7–8	40, 45
5:20	60

Jude	
4	59
5	59
12	53

Revelation	
12:18	73–4
13:7	47

The following passages are discussed in the Postscript: